GIBBON AND ROME

GIBBON AND ROME

by

E. J. OLIVER

SHEED AND WARD
LONDON AND NEW YORK

FIRST PUBLISHED 1958
BY SHEED AND WARD LTD.
33 MAIDEN LANE
LONDON W.C.2
AND
SHEED AND WARD, INC.
840 BROADWAY
NEW YORK 3

B
G o

PRINTED IN GREAT BRITAIN
BY PURNELL AND SONS, LTD.
PAULTON (SOMERSET) AND LONDON

To

NIGEL DENNIS

With the natural humility of a Christian bent
on preserving his identity in face of a lion

ACKNOWLEDGEMENT

Quotations from Miss J. E. Norton's *The Letters of Edward Gibbon* are here reproduced by kind permission of the author and Messrs. Cassell and Company.

CONTENTS

CONTENTS

I

ARCHITECTURE AMONG THE RUINS

. . . I can neither forget nor express the strong emotions which agitated my mind as I first approached and entered the eternal city. (Gibbon, *Autobiography*, p. 158.)[1]

THE calm landscape of the eighteenth century, with its noble perspectives of columns and arches, temples and pavilions, has the fascination of tranquillity and permanence to those who gaze back from scenes clouded with the heat of revolutions and the smoke of bombs. Yet before that century ended it was itself shaken by two great revolutions—the American, which some even then saw as the decline of the British Empire, and the French, which achieved the downfall of the Holy Roman Empire.

Both these revolutions, whose effects have spread across the world and whose dates are still celebrated on the calendar, had already shown their strength before the historian of the Roman Empire, Edward Gibbon, had been laid to rest in the year 1794, beneath an appropriately florid Latin inscription, in a Sussex vault.

Although he foresaw the importance of America and the damage which the French would inflict on the stability of Europe, his serenity had not been unduly troubled by these revolutions. Yet his nearest connections were in England, in French-speaking Switzerland, or in France herself, and while indolent by habit he was ready enough to put himself out on

[1] A note on the editions used is given on p. 195

behalf of his friends. For his own part he bore suffering with equanimity and with cheerfulness, voicing no apprehension even on the day of his death.

In that plump figure, in that face, whose ugliness had so vexed him as a young man, before it had acquired the distinction and the placidity of the historian, there was a serenity which viewed personal misfortunes and public disasters with the same ironical detachment. Yet he was not insensitive. The alertness and the amusement in his large eyes redeemed the commonplace features, which had been compared to a potato, while the large button of a nose, which drew in such quantities of snuff, had the sensitive precision of a terrier's, in extracting the bone of fact from the ashheap of history.

This serenity, which so marked the mind and the person of Edward Gibbon, was certainly a characteristic of his age, and it was deeper in him precisely because he was so perfect a representative of his century. The virtues of the period were incarnate in him; the irony, the confidence, the proportion. As French classical drama has the lucidity and order which also created the architecture of Versailles, so the sentences of Gibbon have the loftiness and the calm exhibited in the great country houses of England.

It is natural to turn to architecture when considering Gibbon and his age, for it is the most enduring of the arts which reflects their qualities. Their respect was given to what survived, to the heritage of civilization. If they were not disposed to believe in the permanence of emotion, whether this was aroused by a woman or by a religion, nor had faith in the institutions which were changing or decaying around them, they had the greater reverence for the amenities, the arts, and the elegance which they had inherited or recovered from the past. Their own architecture was consciously modelled on classical standards, and it was a consequence of this that the end of the century should be conspicuous for the building of roads and the taking of baths, two great arts of the Roman Empire. There was an almost Chinese formality in this respect for ancestral qualities, which also expressed itself in admiration for the arts and civilization of China. The cult of ruins further revealed this reverence for architecture and for the columns of the past.

Yet this respect was entirely distinct from the historical passion of the nineteenth century or the archaeological enthusiasm of the twentieth, which have attempted to distinguish and to contrast the epochs of the past, so leading to the division of history, art, and myth into cycles of development and decay, emphasizing the effects of time, whose subtleties have so engaged the contemporary mind.

The eighteenth century had no such anxiety about the nature of time. However deep was its scepticism on ultimate causes or the claims of religion, it had no doubts on the value of civilization or of human experience, for even when it affected to admire and even to practise the simple life and primitive virtues, it so retained its own habits that its noble savage was recognizably related to Marie Antoinette's rustic arbours— neither of them out of touch with the classical columns of civilization.

There was still a strong sense of the unity of mankind, to which the revolutionaries could appeal in proclaiming the brotherhood and equality of men—a unity which extended over time and space, so that chronicles of travel, such as those of Captain Cook (who was almost as representative of the eighteenth century as Gibbon himself), were as much appreciated as works of history; not, as today, for their contrast with ordinary experience, but for the evidence they brought of other relations in the human family.

With remarkable self-confidence the eighteenth century adapted the ruins of the past to its own uses and refashioned

3

ancient masterpieces in its own style. Italian madonnas could still wear the clothes of daily life, Garrick could play Shakespeare in the same coat as he wore in the street, Pope could translate Homer into an eighteenth-century epic, in which the goddesses posed as naturally as in the park of an English country gentleman. The historical sense of later generations has accorded smiles or scorn to these artifices, but it was just this lack of a historical sense which sustained the bright and equable climate of the eighteenth century.

It might even be claimed that this timeless element gave to the men of that age a more vivid sense of the past, for if they were not always able to understand the passions or the beliefs of those long dead, they at least acknowledged them as contemporaries, men with motives and aspirations not too different from their own. They had a familiarity with their ancestors which perhaps comes less easily to those who are more alertly aware of the difference between past and present.

It was in this timeless climate, among the ruins which are the point of rest in so many eighteenth-century landscapes, that the serenity of Edward Gibbon developed, giving him the calm necessary to his life's work, the study of the Roman Empire in its decline and fall. Much of the charm of that great work may well be due, not only to its erudition and style, admirable and rare though these are, but also, and even more, to its unity and smoothness of texture, which arise directly from the timeless climate in which it was composed. If on its first appearance it was read as eagerly as a novel, this was because it created that illusion of suspended time in which the novel seeks to preserve the mortal emotions of its characters.

Gibbon judged events in the history of Rome with the serenity and the detachment of a scholar, but it was with these same qualities that he observed events in London which took place in his own life-time. The tone of a letter of his

4

ARCHITECTURE AMONG THE RUINS

(6 June 1780), on the Gordon Riots, which happened when he was in London, was little different from that of a passage in *The Decline and Fall* (v, p. 136) on religious disturbances in the fifth century when "in pursuit of a metaphysical quarrel, many thousands were slain and the Christians of every degree were deprived of the substantial enjoyments of social life". (ch. xlvii). He observed both with as much or as little partiality.

He had prejudices such as afflict all mankind, but despite his confidence in the merits of his own age, he lacked that most persistent of prejudices which seeks to draw only lessons from the past and transforms the dead into ghosts to frighten children. Uncorrupted by the spirit of time, he regarded the dead and the living with an equal justice. That he also observed them with equal prejudice is only one more illustration of the unity which he imposed on past and present time.

It is this timeless element which gives a special interest to the words set at the head of this chapter, recording the "strong emotions" with which he entered the *"eternal city"*. That Rome had long been so described does not diminish the emphasis which he gave to the phrase, for he was not a writer to repeat a commonplace which could not support his own shade of meaning, and few have chosen words with more care. He gravitated to Rome precisely because it was the centre of a timeless world most congenial to his spirit. It was in that city, where classical architecture survived among the ruins, that he conceived his most impressive vision of the fabric of history, woven without a seam.

"It was at Rome," he wrote in his autobiography (p. 160) in words that have been read and repeated by every lover of Gibbon "on the 15th of October, 1764, as I sat musing amidst the ruins of the Capitol . . . that the idea of writing the decline

5

and fall of the city first started to my mind. But my original plan was circumscribed to the decay of the city rather than of the empire . . ."

When, over twenty years later, he wrote the final pages of this greater history—Chapter LXXI—it was to the ruins of Rome that his mind returned, and he devoted his last words to examining the causes of their decay and survival, noting with satisfaction any happy chance which had contributed to preserve them. There were no earthquakes: "The air and earth have doubtless been shaken; and the lofty turrets of Rome have tottered from their foundations; but the seven hills do not appear to be placed on the great cavities of the globe; nor has the city, in any age, been exposed to the convulsions of nature, which, in the climate of Antioch, Lisbon, or Lima, have crumbled in a few moments the works of ages into dust." (vii, p. 318.)

He was even able to find some indulgence for Christian bishops, in consideration of their part in conserving the city: "Of the Christian hierarchy, the bishops of Rome were commonly the most prudent and least fanatic; nor can any positive charge be opposed to the meritorious act of saving and converting the majestic structure of the Pantheon." (vii, p. 322.) A Christian cleric, Dean Milman, found this indulgence excessive, adding a footnote in his edition, to observe that the popes, in earlier times, had no power to dispose of the city's monuments.

In this same chapter Gibbon repeated the proverbial expression, recorded by Bede: "As long as the Coliseum stands, Rome shall stand; when the Coliseum falls, Rome will fall; when Rome falls, the world will fall" (vii, p. 330), noting that it should be ascribed to Anglo-Saxons pilgrims who had visited Rome before Bede's death, more than a thousand years before Gibbon's own visit.

6

Nor did he neglect more recent buildings, also listing "the dome of St. Peter, the most glorious structure that ever has been applied to the use of religion". (vii, p. 337.)

In his final sentence he returned to his first vision: "It was among the ruins of the Capitol that I first conceived the idea of a work which has amused and exercised near twenty years of my life . . ." (vii, p. 338.)

"The ruins of the Capitol"—the phrase recurs in the autobiography as in the history, two works joined not only by the same magnificence and idiosyncrasy of style, but by the same inspiration, that of Rome, which aroused such strong emotions in the decisive moment of his life, which was evoked with such majesty in the pages of *The Decline and Fall*. Rome was his grand passion, occupying that central position in his being which no woman and no religion were able to maintain, perhaps, too, drawing to herself some of that love and faith which critics of Gibbon have found wanting in his personal life and in his intellectual structure.

When recently the sumptuous and definitive edition of Gibbon's letters was published by Miss J. E. Norton, some critics, in appreciating the work, professed to find a lack of warmth in his character. This might be justified from a perusal of the letters, for nobody was further than Gibbon from the relaxed mood, the slippers, and convivial glass of a Charles Lamb or other writers who are more themselves in their letters than in their books. As he said in the first page of his autobiography, ". . . style is the image of character; and the habits of correct writing may produce, without labour or design, the appearance of art and study." He always dressed with scrupulous correctness, and he showed the same deference to public taste, though not to public opinion, when he wrote history. The habit persisted in the writing of letters as in the composing of memoirs, for the unity between his private and his public

7

life was no less complete than that between his attitude to history and to public events in his own lifetime.

So his letters have all the serenity of the historian, but they have less interest than *The Decline and Fall* because their subject matter is often trivial. He was, too, a reluctant letter-writer. Often he accused himself of dilatoriness in his correspondence. He was the type of writer who, daily exercising his pen on serious work, grudges the waste of it on personal topics, and refuses to make it the instrument of gossip. Even so, it is difficult to read his letters without receiving a strong impression of the sincerity of his affections and the friendliness and courtesy of his character.

This is the same impression which often lingers with readers of *The Decline and Fall*. Gibbon is a pleasing writer because he is a consistent one. His good manners are as evident in his writing as they were in his life. He never raises the tone of his voice, describing the most barbarous scenes with the same urbanity as he details the civilized structures of Rome or of Byzantium. The unity of the man and the material is constantly apparent, and he is himself the most civilized of writers.

His treatment reinforces the effect of timelessness. In Chapter X of *The Decline and Fall*, he spoke of "pursuing not so much the doubtful arrangement of dates as the more natural distribution of subjects". (i, p. 274.) Two chapters later, in another protest against the tyranny of time, he referred to Tacitus—with whom Sheridan once linked the name of Gibbon—as "the philosophic historian whose writings will instruct the last generations of mankind". (i, p. 344.) As when he observed the ruins of Rome, his respect was most firmly held by the durable and the permanent.

Poets, from Shakespeare and Ronsard to a host of lesser men, have pleaded with their mistresses to grant them favours on the grounds that they alone can defy the ravages of time, that beauty will survive in their "eternal lines". On a June night in 1787 when Gibbon had set down the last line of his history ". . . a sober melancholy was spread over my mind, by the idea that I had taken an everlasting leave of an old and agreeable companion, and that whatsoever might be the future date of my *History*, the life of the historian must be short and precarious". (*Autobiography*, p. 205.) This poetic vanity in the "future date" of his work, which would survive the passage of time, returned to him in the last pages of his autobiography, when he remarked that an author might be gratified "that one day his mind will be familiar to the grandchildren of those who are yet unborn". (p. 219.)

The same opposition to time has been frequently noted as a characteristic of his work. It is one of the grand merits of *The Decline and Fall of the Roman Empire* that it imposes its unity upon the centuries. Madame Necker, who as a girl had been Gibbon's only love, was the first to employ an image which has been often repeated since, when she spoke of it as "this bridge which joins the ancient world to the modern". Carlyle hardly varied the terms when he referred to it as "a kind of bridge that connects the antique with the modern ages". Mr. G. M. Young, in recalling these images, added one more exact when he called it "a Roman aqueduct".

Once more it is towards architecture that the appreciation of Gibbon turns—architecture, which is man's most enduring protest against the oblivion of time, the nearest he has come, whether in Ur of the Chaldees, in Knossos, in the Maya erections of Yucatan, or in Rome herself, to establishing an "eternal city" on this earth. But there is a deeper interest in the fact that these remarks should so persistently return to the image of a bridge, for at Rome the *Pontifex Maximus* was, literally, the "maker of bridges", a title which still survives in that of the Roman Pontiff. In building his own bridge of reason and learning across the centuries, Gibbon naturally came into opposition to the Roman Church, which stood alone in claiming the same right to connect the ancient and the modern worlds.

Gibbon was never more truly Roman than when he was defending Rome against the infiltration of the Christians. To him they were the same dangerous revolutionaries as had vexed the temper of the most equable emperors, whom he so admired —even the serene Marcus Aurelius, of whom Gibbon wrote in Chapter XVI of *The Decline and Fall*: "During the whole course of his reign Marcus despised the Christians as a philosopher, and punished them as a sovereign." (ii, p. 116.)

Some readers may feel that Gibbon himself thought and behaved not very differently, for his references to the Christian religion are generally ironical, while he sometimes uses the sovereign right of a historian to judge the dead, by condemning the Christians and their clergy—"a celebrated order of men which has furnished the most important, though not always the most edifying, subjects for modern history." (ii, p. 50: ch. xv.)

Many reasons have been put forward to explain his famous attitude towards Christianity, some of them developing Macaulay's remark that he was like a man who had received a personal injury from it, and arguing that his conversion to the Roman Church, in whose communion he remained for eighteen months as a very young man, had left some sort of bitterness behind it. Mr. Christopher Dawson, in his introduction to the "Everyman" edition of *The Decline and Fall*—perhaps the most illuminating essay written on Gibbon—rejects this explanation and suggests that it was due to the "intellectual discomfort" caused by the intervention in his history of the religious element, which distorted his narrative, because he could not find a place for it in his philosophy.

Mr. Dawson himself reveals Gibbon's attitude brilliantly when he says: "He felt as a Roman; he thought as a Roman; he wrote as a Roman."

This is to go back to Marcus Aurelius and justify the claim that Gibbon's attitude to Christianity was little different from that of the Roman emperors who regarded it as a threat to the established order and to the civil administration of their empire. It was Gibbon's Roman piety towards the Eternal City which led him to defend it against that other city "not made with hands".

Here the question of Gibbon and Rome reveals its wider aspect, that of the permanent tension between the policy of governments and the spirit of religion. To Gibbon, Rome and the classical tradition stood for eternal elements of reason and order, in serenity of mind and in the government of men. In Chapter III of *The Decline and Fall* he wrote: "If a man were called to fix the period in the history of the world, during which the condition of the human race was most happy and prosperous, he would, without hesitation, name that which elapsed from the death of Domitian to the accession of Commodus." (i, pp. 85–6.) This golden age, lasting less than a century, ended in A.D. 180, but to Gibbon it remained the measure of human felicity. It included the rule of the two Antonines, of whom he wrote in the same chapter: "Their united reigns are possibly the only period of history in which the happiness of a great people was the sole object of government." (i, p. 84.)

This was also the period chosen by Walter Pater as the setting for his beautiful vision of the early Christian Church in *Marius the Epicurean*, where the chapel in Cecilia's house conceals a mystery unknown to the urbane talkers of the forum—among whom may be included Gibbon himself, for it was a part of his timeless quality that he was no less critical of

Christianity in its primitive form than of that which it assumed in his own age.

It is this which gives a special interest to his attitude, as it is more usual for critics of Christianity to reject it in their own time, while recognizing its merits in other periods—in Evangelical or Puritan movements, in Spanish mystics, in Florentine art, in the Middle Ages, in the earlier centuries, in the Apostolic age, or perhaps only at the moment when the Sermon on the Mount was preached.

Gibbon was more consistent, because he was not affected by the spirit of time. If he would have preferred to live in the age of the Antonines, at least he did not live very differently in his own day; as a philosopher, as a senator, as a historian, he retained the dignity and the piety of a Roman.

The clarity of his mind and his language reveal how naturally his devotion to Rome led him into opposition to Christianity, but they also illuminate the attitude of many others who have not stated their views so clearly. There has long been, for instance, in English university life, a tradition of irony towards Christianity which arises from the same cause, the same loyalty towards Rome and the classical tradition. More than one generation of scholars, in the proudest age of the British Empire, had a Roman scorn for the followers of the crucified God. But the reasons for that scorn are all better set out in Gibbon. There is the contempt for Christian writers who debased the language of Cicero, for poets whose verses limped so painfully behind Horace, for historians who could not approach the dignity of Livy. There is the masculine distaste, reinforced by a Puritan ancestry, for a religion which not only admits a feminine presence to its altars, but even decorates them with tinsel and paint. There is the scholar's aloofness from displays of popular emotion and religious fervour. But dominating these matters of taste there is the stronger conviction that the great task of life is the government of men, not speculations about the other world, still less the addressing of petitions to it.

This attitude towards Christianity was not confined to Britain, nor was Gibbon himself most influenced by English writers. In France, where the Roman tradition was stronger, there had long been a tension between the political and the Christian interpretation of it, while in Italy and the German lands the struggle between the Empire and the Papacy turned on the same theme.

It even remains a contemporary question, this tension between the Roman tradition, which Gibbon so magnificently celebrated, and the Christian; for with the French Revolution and the growth of nationalism the Roman ideal of the Government as the supreme authority was asserted by the French under Napoleon, by the Italians under Cavour, by the Germans under Bismarck and again under Hitler. These nationalists despised and at times even persecuted the Christians, on the same grounds as under the Roman Empire: that they were a menace to the order and authority of the State.

But although these national states had a similar attitude towards the Christians, they more resembled the barbarians in that they were themselves an offence against the unity and the Roman peace which had been the achievement of the imperial authority in its greatest age, regarded by Gibbon with so much respect. In a letter written in the year before his death he himself described the French revolutionaries as "the most dangerous fanatics that have ever invaded the peace of Europe". He was loyal to the Roman Empire as a principle of unity and authority, but in the later conflict of nations, as in the earlier combats of the barbarians, it was the Christian tradition which stood for unity.

Gibbon was quite aware of this, for in Chapter LXI of
The Decline and Fall he wrote:

> The authority of the priests operated in the darker ages
> as a salutary antidote: they prevented the total extinction
> of letters, mitigated the fierceness of the times, sheltered the
> poor and defenceless, and preserved or revived the peace
> and order of civil society. But the independence, rapine,
> and discord of the feudal lords were unmixed with any
> semblance of good . . . (vi, p. 465.)

His first impressions of the revolutionaries associated them
with these feudal lords, for in the last pages of his *Autobiography* (p. 216) he declared:

> I beg leave to subscribe my assent to Mr. Burke's creed
> on the revolution of France. I admire his eloquence, I
> approve his politics, I adore his chivalry, and I can almost
> excuse his reverence for church establishments. I have
> sometimes thought of writing a dialogue of the dead, in
> which Lucian, Erasmus, and Voltaire should mutually
> acknowledge the danger of exposing an old superstition to
> the contempt of the blind and fanatic multitude.

If Gibbon could almost excuse Burke's "reverence for
church establishments", this was because he had himself so
much respect for civil establishments that he was at moments
obliged to admire those elements of order and unity which the
Church had inherited from the civil administration of the
Roman Empire. In Chapter LXIX of *The Decline and Fall*
he noted that "the ecclesiastical power that was obeyed in
Sweden and Britain had been ultimately derived from the
suffrage of the Romans". (vii, p. 221.) Again, in Chapter

XLIX he had used words which would better suit the fervour of a medievalist: "The republic of Europe, with the pope and emperor at its head." (v, p. 330*n*.)

However ready he was to amuse himself and his readers at the expense of the Christians and their clergy, he was unable to suppress his respect for Rome, even when it was in their hands. In the penultimate chapter of *The Decline and Fall*, Chapter LXX, he pleasantly united these feelings to say: "For myself, it is my wish to depart in charity with all mankind, nor am I willing, in these last moments, to offend even the pope and clergy of Rome." (vii, p. 331.)

To English readers—as also to Eastern Europeans—more accustomed in their literature to praise for the pure spirit of Christianity and attacks on the corruption of Rome, there is something unexpected in Gibbon's reversal of this to ironical remarks on the Christians and respectful tributes to Rome. Nor was this only due to his scepticism, for he was at least as influenced by genuine devotion to Rome as by distaste for religion.

A philosopher of the seventeenth century, Thomas Hobbes, as famous a sceptic as Gibbon, had observed the ruins of Rome with different eyes when he delivered his great judgment: "For what is the Papacy but the ghost of the Roman Empire sitting crowned on the grave thereof?" A Papist himself might applaud the majesty and the element of historical truth in this conception, while Gibbon delivered a similar judgment acceptable equally to philosophers and to Christians when he recalled in Chapter XV of *The Decline and Fall*: "It has been observed, with truth as well as propriety, that the conquests of Rome prepared and facilitated those of Christianity." (ii, p. 60.)

It is evident that Gibbon saw, no less clearly than Hobbes, that Christianity had grown out of the Roman Empire, yet for him "the ghost of the Roman Empire" was so mighty a shade that he would never have let it rest in the hands of the Christians. If to Hobbes the chief Christian bishopric was the natural heir of the Roman Empire, to Gibbon it was more the assassin of that empire, inheriting something of its majesty indeed, but haunted only by the ghost of its victim.

Yet even his irony, so ready to tease the Christians, becomes gentler when he approaches his beloved Rome, and almost permits a legend to escape his censure. In Chapter XXXV, recording that Attila was dissuaded from Rome, he mentioned the apparition of the two Apostles, St. Peter and St. Paul, in defence of the city, as "one of the noblest legends", to add that "some indulgence is due to a fable, which has been represented by the pencil of Raphael". (iii, p. 500.) More, he had indulgence enough to insert in a footnote that this legend was "rejected, however, by the most learned and pious Catholics"—a surprising concession, for he was not accustomed to associate learning with piety.

In fact this great historian, who has appeared to some as a man cold in nature and cynical in philosophy, had his great passion, but it was that of a scholar, and it was centred on a Rome that was neither Italian nor Christian, but simply Roman —the "eternal city" which, alone of mortal things, had aroused his "strong emotions".

Gibbon is not the only man of letters to be so inspired by Rome and to shun the company of Christians, for there are ancient statues in the centre of the city and in the centre of our civilization which have never received a Christian imprint. European literature can show many writers whose inspiration is Roman and classical, but not Christian in spirit, especially among the French and Italians of the last century, though a few English aesthetes have followed De Quincey in combining an interest in the Roman emperors with more toxic pleasures.

ARCHITECTURE AMONG THE RUINS

But of all those whom Rome has inspired, Gibbon surely has responded with most dignity both to her splendour and to her persistence.

Perhaps the most interesting commentary on Gibbon's Roman antipathy to Christianity is provided by the views of another writer of genius, himself a Latin from the heart of Roman France—Charles Maurras, who erected his zeal for Rome and the classical tradition into a coherent philosophy of politics which had a considerable influence on European intellectuals in the first half of the present century.

For Maurras the Roman tradition was not simply the historical framework in which Christianity had developed, but the vital essence of it, salvaged from its Jewish past and to be defended against the "barbarians", among whom he numbered democrats, liberals, Communists, Socialists, and those Christians who were outside the communion of Roman authority. Maurras, though not a believer himself, championed the Roman Church simply because he saw it as "the ghost of the Roman Empire". Because he to some extent represented a Catholic political reaction against anti-clerical governments, he achieved a large Catholic following, which only dwindled when his paper, the organ of French royalism, was condemned by the Vatican.

Maurras provides an interesting contrast to Gibbon's opposition between the Roman and the Christian traditions, for he refused to separate them, as Gibbon refused to reconcile them. Nor is this a simple contrast between a Frenchman and an Englishman, for Gibbon was himself soaked in French culture and even wrote his first work in French. It is perhaps more a contrast between a historian who had disengaged himself from the spirit of time and a polemist who wrote daily with the needs and events of his own age constantly in mind. But both Gibbon and Maurras identified Rome with civilization,

GIBBON AND ROME

finding in her eternity an inspiration which is more commonly sought in the other world.

Certainly Gibbon was the finer exponent of the classical and Roman tradition, but how far even he, who so situated himself in a timeless element, was also influenced by the circumstances of his own life and the atmosphere of his own age, to the prejudice of the Christian tradition, it will be the main purpose of this study to examine.

II

THE PERPETUAL SOURCE

The love of study, a passion which derives fresh vigour from enjoyment, supplies each day, each hour, with a perpetual source of independent and rational pleasure. . . .

(Autobiography, p. 218.)

IT is characteristic of Gibbon that on first sitting down to compose his memoirs he should discourse at some length— in proportion to his whole narrative—not only of his ancestors, but of the general love of antiquity and lineage in the hearts of mankind. This fondness for general principles he shared with his age, but on the matter of heredity it was reinforced in him by respect for tradition: "The satirist may laugh, the philosopher may preach; but reason herself will respect the prejudices and habits, which have been consecrated by the experience of mankind." *(Autobiography,* p. 2.)

Yet his pride as a man of letters led him to question the popular prejudice in favour of royal descent, for "in the estimate of honour we should learn to value the gifts of nature above those of fortune . . . and to pronounce the descendant of a king less truly noble than the offspring of a man of genius, whose writings will instruct or delight the latest posterity." (p. 3.) He went on to tell the clan of the Spencers and the Churchills that they should take more pride in the *Faery Queen* of Edmund Spenser than in the triumphs of the great Duke of Marlborough, while the Fieldings, Earls of Denbigh, should be more flattered by their relation to the Henry Fielding who wrote *Tom Jones* than by their connection with the Hapsburgs. It is even more certain, a reflective reader may observe, that Edward Gibbon, the historian of the Roman Empire, was the noblest of the Gibbons.

But perhaps the chief interest of Gibbon's introductory remarks is his reference to the civilization of China:

> The family of Confucius is, in my opinion, the most illustrious in the world. After a painful ascent of eight or ten centuries, our barons and princes of Europe are lost in the darkness of the middle ages; but, in the vast equality of the empire of China, the posterity of Confucius have maintained, above two thousand two hundred years, their peaceful honours and perpetual succession. The chief of the family is still revered, by the sovereign and the people, as the lively image of the wisest of mankind.
>
> *(Autobiography, p. 3.)*

Here once more Gibbon was in his timeless element, and he could view the Celestial Empire in the perspective of the Roman, while the British Empire itself was developing a civil service similar to the Chinese, in which the great Whig families served as the mandarins.

But Gibbon suffered from the disadvantage of a Tory ancestry, for the Tory party was still tainted in the eighteenth century by the memory of its dubious loyalty to the House of Hanover, until reconstructed towards the end of the century into the new conservative grouping of the younger Pitt. Gibbon himself, as a man of his age, accepted the new dynasty, but he wrote with affection of his immediate Tory ancestors and with pride of his more remote forebears.

The Gibbons came originally from the county of Kent, where they already held land in the fourteenth century, and one of them was architect to King Edward the Third. The elder branch of the family remained in Kent in a state of "golden mediocrity", but at the beginning of the seventeenth century a younger branch moved into the City of London, where Gibbon's grandfather, who was born in 1666, the year of the Great Fire, accumulated a fortune in trade, becoming in the year 1716 one of the directors of the South Sea Company—though even before that date he had amassed sixty thousand pounds.

The South Sea Company had a monopoly of trade with South America and the Pacific islands, and in 1719 it proposed to take over the National Debt in return for further concessions. There was an outbreak of speculation which sent its hundred-pound shares up to a thousand. The old illusions of fabulous wealth and El Dorado seized the City of London. The Tories took particular delight in the Company, regarding it as a rival to the Bank of England, the darling of the Whigs, which offered five million for a concession, but was outbid by a still larger offer from the Company. Other companies were formed, though the South Sea Company used its influence to have numbers of them declared illegal. When their own stock reached the grossly inflated figure of a thousand, the directors sold out five million of their shares. Then, in 1720, what became known as the South Sea Bubble burst with a shock that ruined many investors.

In his *Autobiography* (p. 12) Gibbon makes no reference to these details, on the plea that "of the guilt or innocence of my grandfather and his brother directors, I am neither a competent nor a disinterested judge". But he argued with reason that the proceedings instituted against the directors were at least as questionable as their own, for a bill of pains and penalties was introduced which was retrospective in its effects, punishing offences which were not illegal when they were committed, and the defendants were refused a hearing—two abuses of justice. They were also prevented from leaving the country and forced to render an exact account of the value of their estates. As over a hundred members in the House of Commons were debtors of the Company, it is further evident that they were hardly disinterested judges of the affair.

The Chancellor of the Exchequer, John Aislabie, was expelled from the House and imprisoned. Gibbon's grandfather declared on oath that his fortune amounted to over a hundred thousand pounds, of which he was allowed to retain ten thousand. On this remnant he proceeded to build a new fortune which before his death reached a figure comparable with the old, but he divided this between his two daughters and the son, who was Gibbon's father.

One of these daughters, Hester, took into her household William Law, who ranks with Mother Julian of Norwich among the greatest of English mystics. Law was a non-juror, one of those who refused to take the oath to the House of Hanover, on which Gibbon remarks that "the sacrifice of interest to conscience will be always respectable". It was a sacrifice not frequently made in eighteenth-century England, and some have held that the non-jurors were the most devout representatives of religion there before the coming of Wesley. Certainly Law was the greatest of all, and his writings are still full of life. Mr. Aldous Huxley, who, in his *Perennial Philosophy*, has set together quotations from the mystics of all countries and all ages, has perhaps drawn on Law more deeply than on any other writer in English. Gibbon himself, whose historical mind had no tincture of mysticism, unless it was on the subject of Rome, conceded of Law that "had not his vigorous mind been clouded by enthusiasm, he might be ranked with the most agreeable and ingenious writers of the times". (*Autobiography*, p. 16.)

THE PERPETUAL SOURCE

One of the reasons which made Gibbon—and indeed many others, Christian preachers among them—most critical of Christians, was the contrast between the professions of their faith and the conduct of their daily lives, as the zeal for gain or pleasure is often more visible than preoccupation with the other world, and there is always a tendency "to beat the breast of one's neighbour in penitence for sin". Here Law was able to satisfy Gibbon, who admitted that "a philosopher must allow that he exposes, with equal severity and truth, the strange contradiction between the faith and practice of the Christian world".

Gibbon's father, who was born in 1707, had Law as his tutor at home in Putney, but he also went to Westminster and Cambridge. Afterwards he made the Grand Tour and, falling ill at Besançon, he was attended by one of the Actons who had studied medicine. The Gibbons were related to the Acton family three generations back. This Acton settled down at Besançon, married, and became a Catholic. He was also the great-grandfather of Lord Acton, the historian, so that the two names are now linked not only by blood, but by scholarship.

After Gibbon's father had returned to England, he was elected, in 1734, to Parliament, where he usually voted with the Tories and against Sir Robert Walpole, who had taken a lead in the proceedings against the South Sea Company.

Gibbon himself was born three years later in Putney, on 27th April, according to the old calendar which England still retained at that date, in the year 1737, the eldest son of his mother, Judith, who also bore five other sons and one daughter, all of whom died in childhood, the fate of at least half those born in that period. The daughter lived long enough for Gibbon to remember her as "an amiable infant", and he regretted the loss of a sister who might perhaps have been the relation most agreeable to his bachelor nature. The remark he

makes in this connection, admirably exact in itself, may also
help to explain why he never married:

> The relation of a brother and a sister, especially if they
> do not marry, appears to me of a very singular nature. It
> is a familiar and tender friendship with a female, much about
> our own age; an affection perhaps softened by the secret
> influence of sex, but pure from any mixture of sensual desire,
> the sole species of Platonic love that can be indulged with
> truth, and without danger. (*Autobiography*, p. 19.)

"Without danger"—that may suggest the caution of a
bachelor, but the whole passage also reveals his capacity for
affection and for friendship.

That affection is no less evident in the tones in which he
speaks of his mother's sister, Catherine Porten, the aunt to
whom he owed the happiest hours of his childhood, and
perhaps his life, for he was a sickly child, and she nursed him
through his sufferings. His mother died when he was only
ten, and both her social duties and her husband had kept her
from her son, who also records that her attention "was somewhat diverted by her frequent pregnancies".

"But the maternal office was supplied by my aunt . . . at
whose name I feel a tear of gratitude trickling down my cheek."
(*Autobiography*, p. 21.) In Gibbon, as in other intellectual
natures of his sort, there is sometimes an apparent contrast
between a cynicism in weighing human motives and a sudden
warmth of affection, but possibly the two qualities are more
closely joined than always appears: it was just because he saw
so deeply into human pretences and self-deceptions that he
was so moved and so grateful when he met with genuine
emotion. The same contrast occurs in *The Decline and Fall*
when, after he has exposed the vanities or inadequacies of

generals or bishops, he suddenly pays tribute to the nobler qualities of a Belisarius or an Athanasius.

Certainly there can be no doubt of the sincerity of his devotion to Catherine Porten nor of hers to him: "Many wakeful nights did she sit by my bedside in trembling expectation that each hour would be my last. Of the various and frequent disorders of my childhood my own recollection is dark; nor do I wish to expatiate on so disgusting a topic." (*Autobiography*, p. 21.) It has since been conjectured that these disorders were a form of infantile rheumatism.

The pains and sufferings of youth had not yet made their entry into literature when Gibbon was a boy. Rousseau had still to expose the art of confession, and Europe had still to weep over the sufferings of young Werther and of Goethe. Gibbon maintained a Roman discipline on such disgusting topics, but even he confessed to the misery of school, which has been treated in so many novels since—the swift removal from the comforts and affections of home "to the frugal diet and strict subordination of a school . . . to the rude familiarity of his equals, the insolent tyranny of his seniors, and the rod, perhaps, of a cruel and capricious pedagogue". (*Autobiography*, p. 24.) But even in this recital of woes he kept with classical restraint to the facts.

The shadows of the Tory past continued to hang over him. His tutor before he went to school had been an excellent teacher who one day, reading prayers in the parish church, "most unluckily forgot the name of King George", and had in consequence to be dismissed. So at school in 1746, the year after the rising which had taken Charles Stuart as far as Derby, Gibbon was "reviled and buffeted for the sins of my Tory ancestors".

But his education had proceeded in spite of his sickness, and at home he had learnt to read and write and to work out problems of arithmetic with such success that he could hardly remember a time when such knowledge was not native to him. At school, "by the common methods of discipline, at the expense of many tears and some blood, I purchased the knowledge of the Latin syntax"—his first painful step towards the magnificence of Rome.

His holidays and many relapses into sickness were spent in the care of his aunt, and they talked together "like friends of an equal age". It was she who encouraged, presided over, and shared his reading, which soon developed into the passion which is so often the first sign of the born writer or scholar—so often, too, intensified by ill health or isolation from other amusements of childhood. In that sense it is true that Gibbon was mainly self-educated, but despite that he remained strong in gratitude to his aunt: " . . . to her kind lessons I ascribe my early and invincible love of reading, which I would not exchange for the treasures of India." (*Autobiography*, p. 27.)

Among graver studies, the *Arabian Nights* also contributed to his delight, and it was perhaps to them that he owed those gleams of poetry which illuminate *The Decline and Fall* when it moves towards the East, as in Chapter XXXVII when he speaks of "the vast silence of the desert", or of "the stars, which are seldom clouded in the serene sky of Egypt". (iv, p. 77.)

In the spring of 1748, when Gibbon was eleven, his aunt's father went bankrupt, but their Putney house was not sold until the following Christmas, and he spent the year in what he had come to regard as his real home, having the run of the library, where he seized whatever title took his fancy. It was this year, he decided, which was "the most propitious to the growth of my intellectual stature".

In the following year his aunt, moved both by love of her

nephew and the necessity of supporting herself, took charge of a house for boys going to Westminster School, which enabled her to watch over Gibbon, who entered the school at the same time. But his two years there were constantly interrupted by illness, and in 1750, when he was thirteen, she was medically advised to take him to Bath, where a very painful nervous complaint in the legs "was ineffectually opposed by the various methods of bathing and pumping". She had to leave him there for some months in the care of a servant on her return to Westminster.

The next two years were even more unsettled, divided between his father's houses at Buriton in Hampshire and at Putney, a brief interval at Westminster, Bath, and the homes of private tutors. But wherever there were books, and whatever they were, he read—and with the greater freedom because he was indulged as an invalid—until the moment came when the universal appetite of youth at last fixed on history, though this choice itself was inspired by a *Universal History*, each volume of which he absorbed eagerly as it appeared. This led him to seek out the Roman and Greek historians, whom he read as greedily, though still only in translation, so frequently had his education in the classics been interrupted.

From them he advanced into later historical works, which "I devoured like so many novels; and I swallowed with the same voracious appetite the descriptions of India and China, of Mexico and Peru". (*Autobiography*, p. 32.) This liking for books on travel remained with him all his life. In a letter written in 1789, only five years before his death, he declared: "I am greedy of Voyages and travels." He shared to the full this taste of his age, and there are passages in *The Decline and Fall* which gain much from the lucidity of his geography, as in the very first chapter, when with two or three lines he describes the capital feature of Egypt:

GIBBON AND ROME

The Nile flows down the country, above five hundred miles from the tropic of Cancer to the Mediterranean, and marks, on either side, the extent of fertility by the measure of its inundations. (i, p. 27.)

It was this feeling for geography which contributed most to the timeless quality of his history, for those geographical features which were literally as old as the hills were the most enduring of all the monuments of time and presented an even livelier image of eternity than the ruins of Rome herself.

But it was the history of Rome which had already seized on his boy's imagination, and he recorded his delight on finding a volume new to him, when visiting with his father a friend's house in Wiltshire:

To me the reigns of the successors of Constantine were absolutely new; and I was immersed in the passage of the Goths over the Danube when the summons of the dinner-bell reluctantly dragged me from my intellectual feast.

(*Autobiography*, p. 32.)

After this incursion with the Goths into the Roman Empire, Mr. D. M. Low wittily comments, Gibbon "never came out of it again". He was also inspired to read more of Mahomet and the Saracens than he had learnt in the *Arabian Nights*, though he pursued his reading with the same childish eagerness as he had given to that.

Yet the joys of reading did not bring him to idealize his boyhood: "At the conclusion of this first period of my life, I am tempted to enter a protest against the trite and lavish praise of the happiness of our boyish years which is echoed with so much affectation in the world. That happiness I have never known, that time I have never regretted . . ." But he admitted that his constant illness excluded much happiness and that "the felicity of a schoolboy consists in the perpetual motion of thoughtless and playful agility, in which I was never qualified to excel". (*Autobiography*, p. 33.)

It is possible that this protest against the idealization of boyhood was as much directed against cant as based on his own experience. He had a very sharp eye for hypocrisy and, unlike all those who condemn it, he was equally on guard against any signs of it in himself. Some of the sharpest passages in *The Decline and Fall* were similar protests against the idealization of base or very ordinary actions, for he was as quick to detect the illusions of history and romance as he was to expose those which interpret youth and childhood in the light of the ideal.

But it remains true that he experienced few of the joys usually associated with childhood. Even apart from his ill-health, he had little home or family life, and he was repeatedly moved, never settled in security or confidence. In later life he had a talent for friendship, but he had no opportunity to exercise this in boyhood, when some make lasting friendships, and by the time he had reached adolescence he had already developed so peculiarly, or at least so differently from those of his own age, that he had little in common with them.

It may be that this unsettled childhood contributed to that respect for the timeless which he embodied in the history of Rome, because it was precisely at the most uncertain period of it that he fixed on the study of history, finding in that a home which time could no longer corrupt.

Yet he had two joys in his childhood: the affection of his aunt and the love of reading. Both endured. Reading became not only a "perpetual source" of enjoyment but also in a sense his vocation, as it was upon his wide and critical reading that *The Decline and Fall* was based, while his own affection for his aunt was probably the deepest, certainly the most persistent, feeling that he ever had for a woman, the only one to compare with the "strong emotions" evoked in him by Rome.

His aunt had certainly been more to him than his mother, since whose death his father had been increasingly perplexed about the treatment best adapted to such a boy. He was a man of erratic temperament and at this juncture he decided on what his son called "a singular and desperate measure"—to send him, in the year 1752, to Oxford, where he was entered at Magdalen a few days before his fifteenth birthday.

III

OXFORD MONKS

To the University of Oxford *I* acknowledge no obligation;
and she will as cheerfully renounce me for a son, as I am willing
to disclaim her for a mother.

... steeped in port and prejudice among the monks of Oxford.
(Autobiography, pp. 36, 85.)

GIBBON'S career at Oxford, which lasted not much over
a year, as he was removed, by the scandal of his conversion, only a month and a day after his sixteenth birthday,
was strange and eventful, though he described the period as
"the most idle and unprofitable of my whole life". Certainly
it contributed little or nothing to his education, but as has
happened with others who have either wasted their time
there or lightly allowed others to waste it for them, it was
decisive in his development. It may even be argued that Oxford shares with Paris the ancient privilege of nourishing
rebels against her traditions at least as faithfully as upholders
of them, so that even the vipers she nurses in her bosom owe
to her something of the malignity in their poison.

Gibbon's tongue, which could discharge poison with such
magic, did not spare the University of Oxford. Indeed, he
treated her hardly with more indulgence than he gave to the
Christians, nor is it easy entirely to separate his judgment
against Oxford from his antipathy to them. It has been
suggested that, as it was at Oxford that he gained a Christian
faith which he was to renounce, both these were confused for

him in a common aversion; but it was perhaps more their common discrepancy between profession and practice which aroused his scorn.

It is at least evident that Oxford and the Christians were associated in his mind, for it was the clerical hold on Oxford which he most criticized. Many have visited Oxford with the same pious sense of antiquity as has taken others to Rome, but to Gibbon Oxford had none of Rome's eternity and he even used her antiquity as a reproach.

In the meanwhile [he wrote of Oxford and Cambridge] it will be acknowledged that these venerable bodies are sufficiently old to partake of all the prejudices and infirmities of age. The schools of Oxford and Cambridge were founded in a dark age of false and barbarous science; and they are still tainted with the vices of their origin. Their primitive discipline was adapted to the education of priests and monks; and the government still remains in the hands of the clergy, an order of men whose manners are remote from the present world, and whose eyes are dazzled by the light of philosophy. (*Autobiography*, p. 37.)

Later he rejoiced in his escape from "the monks of Oxford". This was a reproach to the venerable clerics, as the English monasteries had been dissolved two hundred and one years before Gibbon's birth. But the hostility of the reference is clear from a passage in Chapter XXXVII of *The Decline and Fall* in which he asserted that "a cruel and unfeeling temper has distinguished the monks of every age and country". (iv, p. 80.)

Yet he had gone up to Oxford with much satisfaction:

In my fifteenth year I felt myself suddenly raised from a boy to a man: the persons, whom I respected as my superiors in age and academical rank, entertained me with every mark of attention and civility; and my vanity was flattered by the velvet cap and silk gown, which distinguish a gentleman-commoner from a plebeian student. A decent allowance, more money than a schoolboy had ever seen, was at my own disposal; and I might command, among the tradesmen of Oxford, an indefinite and dangerous latitude of credit. A key was delivered into my hands, which gave me the free use of a numerous and learned library: my apartment consisted of three elegant and well-furnished rooms in the new building, a stately pile, of Magdalen College. . . .

(Autobiography, pp. 34–5.)

Not only had he this freedom, but he was rapidly and finally freed from the misery of ill-health:

It might now be apprehended that I should continue for life an illiterate cripple: but as I approached my sixteenth year, nature displayed in my favour her mysterious energies: my constitution was fortified and fixed; and my disorders, instead of growing with my growth and strengthening with my strength, most wonderfully vanished.

(Autobiography, p. 30.)

Thereafter he enjoyed normal health, until his addiction to Madeira brought on the gout which was not much less normal to the age—though it was in early manhood that he first acquired the hydrocele which, after years of constant neglect, was destined to end his life. A hydrocele, which is caused by the formation of a transparent fluid around or near the testicles, is a not uncommon ailment among young men and also among those who have passed middle age. It is a condition which is sometimes mistaken for a rupture, and may indeed accompany this. Gibbon's hydrocele has acquired a certain fame in medical annals because, when surgeons were at last permitted to examine and to operate on it, on the eve of his death, they pronounced it "a most extraordinary case". What made it so remarkable was that it had been so long neglected. It is relevant to broach the subject here, because it seems probable that it was precisely his confidence in his health, displayed in the quotation above, which led him to treat the condition so lightly.

There is a further point. Some psychologists maintain that a man's ailments are typical of his character, and it is at least certain that his reactions to them display this. Gibbon's persistent reticence on this subject and his refusal to allow any reference to his hydrocele are evidence of a prudishness which may be related to a slyness in the more scabrous notes of the *Decline and Fall*. A hydrocele may vary in size from that of a walnut to a coconut; his, in the end, was most prodigiously inflated. In his *Autobiography* (p. 166), he noted that his French style "degenerated into a verbose and turgid declamation". It is noteworthy that his body degenerated with a comparable defect.

Yet in the freedom of youth he had reason to feel that all illness was behind him, for he was untroubled by any material or physical disadvantages when he arrived at Oxford. But his education had been alternately neglected and pushed ahead by his own precocious reading, with the result that he had "a stock of erudition that might have puzzled a doctor, and a degree of ignorance of which a schoolboy would have been ashamed". (*Autobiography*, p. 33.)

If this was not a disadvantage to himself, it was at least an unusual preparation for university life, nor had his father's eccentric decision to send him up to Oxford before he had properly been to school made the situation any more regular.

If Oxford at that period was a peculiar sort of university, it is equally true that Gibbon was an oddity as a pupil.

This renders it difficult to judge whether it was his character or that of eighteenth-century Oxford which was more responsible for the failure of his education there and for the scorn with which he afterwards regarded the place. Education in eighteenth-century England, in many grammar schools no less than in the universities, suffered perhaps more from idleness and corruption and prejudice than either before or since. Few indeed are the academic institutions which could look back on that as their golden age.

Richly endowed, some professors and fellows at Oxford devoted the bulk of their time to gossip and sleep, for which they were pleasantly prepared by copious draughts of port or claret. Some of them were like Gibbon's second tutor, Dr. Winchester, who "well remembered that he had a salary to receive, and only forgot that he had a duty to perform". Their interest in public affairs was almost confined to Tory politics. As for religion, "our venerable mother had contrived to unite the opposite extremes of bigotry and indifference". (*Autobiography*, p. 45.)

Gibbon's own college, Magdalen, had an income not much below thirty thousand pounds a year. In comparing it to a Benedictine abbey, such as that at St.-Germain-des-Prés in Paris, he considered the great Benedictine folios and editions of the Fathers, against which Magdalen had nothing comparable to show in scholarship. It was not the wealth to which he objected, but the fact that, having so much leisure and so many opportunities for study, Oxford produced so little.

Gibbon's case against Oxford is a formidable one, but it is difficult to forget that Dr. Johnson, who had come down from Pembroke only twenty-one years before Gibbon went up, when conditions were much the same, laid the basis of his scholarship there, although so cramped by poverty that he had to leave without taking his degree. Johnson regarded the lectures of Bateman at Christ Church so highly that he used to get them at second-hand from a friend, and in after life he always spoke of Oxford with warm affection and respect. But then his deep religious and Jacobite sympathies were more at home there, and he would not have held it against the dons that "their constitutional toasts were not expressive of the most lively loyalty to the House of Hanover", as Gibbon noted without approval.

But Gibbon used the same tone in speaking of Johnson as of Oxford, observing in Chapter LVIII of *The Decline and Fall* " . . . in the notes of Dr. Johnson, the workings of a bigoted, though vigorous mind, greedy of every pretence to hate and persecute those who dissent from his creed". (vi, p. 277*n*.)

This may be enough to indicate that both men were to some extent guided by their opinions in their attitude towards Oxford, and that it was the same reasons which led them to love and to despise it.

This becomes the more probable when Gibbon criticizes the method of instruction at Oxford, which in essence was much the same as that in existence there at the present day. Doubtless there have been many changes: higher standards of scholarship and admission, more control over undergraduates, less drinking, less wealth, less idleness. But it was the tutorial system itself, whereby the student reports weekly to his tutor and retains a large liberty of reading and study on other days, which Gibbon found inadequate. He recalls how he went weekly to his tutor's rooms, much as an undergraduate might go today, and he comments that he found the occasions "equally devoid of profit and pleasure", which is possibly not an unique experience; it may even be that a student as precociously learned as he was might benefit as little today. The difference is that, in his boredom, he excused himself from attending, and "the apology was accepted with a smile", which could hardly be repeated as frequently today as it was then. His second tutor was even laxer, with the result that "the tutor and pupil lived in the same college as strangers to each other".

Yet this same Oxford had been beloved of John Wesley, who overcame any defects in the system by arranging a time-table for each day of the week. But Gibbon, with his contempt for "enthusiasm", was even further from Wesley and his Holy Club than from Johnson.

In blaming Oxford he did not possibly allow enough for his own disposition, which had already advanced some way to that intellectual independence which was to be so strong in him. As he himself had observed that it was his twelfth year, three years before he went up to Oxford, that had contributed most to his "intellectual stature", there was hardly room for normal development later. Perhaps he showed most awareness of the limitations in any teaching system when he noted, in Chapter IV of *The Decline and Fall*, that "the power of in-struction is seldom of much efficacy, except in those happy dispositions where it is almost superfluous". (i, p. 92.)

It was the lack of discipline which he held most against Oxford, a fault inherent in the tutorial system, but one which many have condoned for the liberty of reading and research which it also permits. Gibbon might have prized this, and it was a gain to his own originality that historical gifts were not early blighted by the bleakness of text-books and the tedium of dates; but the change was too abrupt. In missing school, he also missed the benefits of Oxford.

I cannot affect to believe [he wrote of this time] that nature had disqualified me for all literary pursuits. The

37

specious and ready excuse of my tender age, imperfect preparations, and hasty departure, may doubtless be alleged; nor do I wish to defraud such excuses of their proper weight. Yet in my sixteenth year I was not devoid of capacity or application; even my childish reading had displayed an early though blind propensity for books; and the shallow flood might have been taught to flow in a deep channel and a clear stream. In the discipline of a well-constituted academy, under the guidance of skilful and vigilant professors, I should gradually have risen from translations to originals, from the Latin to the Greek classics, from dead languages to living science: my hours would have been occupied by useful and agreeable studies, the wanderings of fancy would have been restrained, and I should have escaped the temptations of idleness, which finally precipitated my departure from Oxford.   (*Autobiography*, pp. 36–7.)

In this idleness he at least followed one Oxford tradition, and in its most habitual form: "The want of experience, of advice, and of occupation, soon betrayed me into some improprieties of conduct, ill-chosen company, late hours, and inconsiderate expense." (*Autobiography*, p. 44.)

These four sorts of imprudence make an interesting list, for if they are habitual to youth, they are also common in men of fashion, and were especially common in the eighteenth century. Yet Gibbon, though in other traits so much a man of fashion and a man of his age, hardly ever indulged in them again. As soon as he was known at all, he was known and even smiled at for the punctiliousness of his conduct and the care with which he chose his company. Acquaintances noted his elaborate discretion with the same affectionate amusement as a more recent generation showed for a similar quality in Henry James. As for "late hours", he afterwards ordered his day with exact regularity, while he was constantly on guard against "inconsiderate expense"—the chief single topic of his letters is worry over mortgages and the desire to relieve his estate of those encumbrances with which it was burdened at the death of his less prudent father.

Evidently Gibbon at Oxford was very different from the judicious figure of later life. This might be true of most young men, yet the majority of them do not so sharply renounce the days of their youth, even though they may smile at them. It is then possible that Gibbon's dislike of Oxford was partly or even largely dictated by a reaction against his character as a young man, and against his opinions (as Oxford was also the scene of his conversion). Looking back in later life, when he wrote his memoirs, he had little sympathy either for that character or for those opinions, with the natural result that he had as little sympathy for Oxford.

His classical tastes in architecture could approve the new libraries of All Souls and Christ Church and the new buildings —"a stately pile"—of his own Magdalen, but he failed to relish the charm of Oxford, which, despite these and its earlier Renaissance and Stuart beauties, is basically medieval. He found little appeal in the "Towery city and branchy between towers", which a century later enchanted Gerard Hopkins, nor would he, of all men, have been inspired by the fact that

. . . these walls are what
He haunted who of all men most sways my spirits to peace.

This reference to Duns Scotus underlines the difference between eighteenth-century Oxford and the city beloved of the Romantics and the Oxford Movement—which Gibbon nevertheless so oddly anticipated by his conversion.

Yet in the picture which Gibbon draws of Oxford there are

traits recognizable to scholars of a later generation. Tory politics have been discussed since, nor has port been banished from the common rooms. One of Gibbon's ablest biographers, James Cotter Morison, himself a fellow of Corpus, writing in 1878, said: "Some Oxonians perhaps could still partly realise the truth of this original picture by their recollections of faint and feeble copies of it drawn from their experience in youthful days."

"In youthful days"—that phrase may be significant, for it is possibly a habit with these Oxonians, Gibbon or Morison, to look back on "regal dons":

> Compact of ancient tales and port
> And sleep—and learning of a sort

belittling them in the interests of a legend—a singular form of nostalgia for the "bad old days". Even Gibbon hastened to add that Oxford had been much changed for the better since his day.

Yet over a century later, Morison was not quite sure of the change. Even today there may be Oxonians still alive who can read Gibbon's description of his first tutor and have their memory vaguely stirred. "His knowledge of the world was confined to the University; his learning was of the last, rather than of the present age; his temper was indolent; his faculties, which were not of the first rate, had been relaxed by the climate . . ." (*Autobiography*, p. 44.) At least they would agree that the relaxing climate of Oxford had not changed.

But if Gibbon could acknowledge no obligation to the University of Oxford, it is more certain that she stands in his debt, and not only for the amiable traits of her character which he painted or caricatured in his memoirs. For Gibbon has himself become a part of the scholastic tradition which he criticized, so markedly that it permits the conjecture whether it did not influence him more than he was aware. Gibbon's blandness and urbanity, his aloofness, his irony, his flashes of malice, his union of literature and learning, his attitude as a man of the world, his Continental airs and his respect for French historical scholarship—all these things in a lesser degree—for there has only been one Gibbon—are more evident in Oxford scholarship than in that of any other seat of learning.

Oxford has also forgiven him his sins against her traditions. So strict a Tory and High Churchman as George Saintsbury has asserted: "One may be perfectly orthodox and yet enjoy the wicked wit . . ." Sir Charles Oman, in defending his Byzantine Empire against Gibbon's scorn, wrote slightingly of historians "whose staple commodity was Gibbon-and-water", which is a tribute to Gibbon's stronger spirit. Oxford, however Tory in outlook, recognized in him a defender of the established order, and as its own faith grew less fervent it found him both a useful outlet for its doubts, and a reassurance that, whatever charges might be brought against the central faith, the Empire—the British, no less than the Roman— at least remained respectable.

So Gibbon came to occupy in academic circles somewhat the position of Rabelais in literature. He had a licence which was gladly accorded to him, but refused to others. The licence itself became a part of the conservatism, for just as the curious student could be diverted from more recent and more question-able writers by the enjoyment of Rabelais, so those with doubts concerning the history of the Church could be directed to Gibbon. It was an academic method of feeding the young with literary wild oats. To read Rabelais and to read Gibbon pre-pared them to become men of the world. It even happened, as the wise instructors foresaw, that while the frankness of

Rabelais purged the grosser humours of youth, so the polished irony of Gibbon enabled young men to pass harmlessly through the fires of infidelity.

Perhaps if Gibbon himself had had his own works to read when he was at Oxford, he too might have passed through his religious crisis and remained in the Church of his youth. Lacking that recourse, he took a singular step—into the Church of Rome.

IV

ROME'S RELIGION

The blind activity of idleness urged me to advance without
armour into the dangerous mazes of controversy; and at the age
of sixteen, I bewildered myself in the errors of the Church of
Rome.   (*Autobiography*, p. 46.)

ADMIRERS and students of Gibbon have tended to regard
his conversion first with astonishment, then with indifference. The astonishment is justified by the contrast with
the subsequent character of his opinions. The indifference is
justified by the youthful and temporary nature of the change
—he was only sixteen when he entered the Roman communion in June 1753, and he remained in it only eighteen
months, until December 1754.

Yet the astonishment requires to be reconciled with the
indifference, for a surprising action in the life of a great man
has its interest, nor does the brevity of the change destroy that
interest; Gibbon's period at Oxford was even shorter, yet there
are some grounds for believing that it had an effect upon him.

Perhaps one reason why his conversion has not aroused
more comment is that the search has been for direct and
positive effects, of which small trace remains. But the indirect
and the destructive effects were considerable. They merit
attention.

Materially, they changed the course of his life, expelling
him from Oxford, and leading to his prolonged stay in French
Switzerland, where he later settled. Spiritually, they stimulated him to examine every form of religious activity with that

caution and irony which have given him the character he still
holds for his readers.

Speculation on the past is a vain enough pursuit, but his
conversion and return acquire a certain importance if it is
considered what Gibbon would have been like without these
qualities or, even more extraordinary, what he would have been
had he remained in the Roman communion—a Catholic
Gibbon is something to wonder at, yet he admitted that he
learnt his irony from Pascal, who did remain in it. What is
clear and outside speculation, is that conversion broadened his
mind. He had been a Catholic; he remained a cosmopolitan.

The candid account of his conversion which Gibbon himself gives in his autobiography explains the reasons for it. What
he fails to reveal is the emotions that accompanied them. He is
as silent on his feelings as elsewhere in his memoirs, except
when speaking of his aunt or of Rome. Emotions, to his
classical temperament, remained a hardly less "disgusting
topic" than illness.

Yet it may be that his conversion was unaccompanied by
emotion, for what is striking in his account is that this was
essentially the conversion of a historian. It was the history of
the Church which led to his conversion, as it was the history of
the Church which later became the object of his criticism. Indeed, it might be argued that there was as little in defence or
attack of what today is more commonly accepted as religion in
the one as in the other. In this perspective there is a real
continuity between Gibbon the Catholic and Gibbon the
critical historian, for both were more concerned with the
historic reality of the Church than with the spirit or even with
the doctrines of Christianity.

So much is clear from Gibbon's own account, which records how he read Middleton's *Free Enquiry* at Oxford: "His
bold criticism, which approaches the precipice of infidelity,

produced on my mind a singular effect . . ." (*Autobiography*, p. 46.) Middleton, in throwing doubt on miracles claimed in the first four or five centuries of Christianity, argued that within the same period "most of the leading doctrines of Popery were already introduced in theory and practice". So Gibbon, retaining his faith in the miracles, found himself obliged to accept Popery with them.

His logical mind saw that miracles, because they insist on the supernatural, are basic to religion. As logically, when he became a sceptic, it was on miracles that he cast his sharpest doubts.

There is an irony in this destructive attack which drove him into the Church, but it is one that has probably been repeated by his own work, which has led some readers at least into sympathy for the Catholic tradition, as he so brands the early Christians with the charges later brought against the Church. Such readers may accept the unity between the early Christians and their Church, yet still differ in their judgment of the realities behind the history.

It is probable that Gibbon was also turned towards Rome by reaction against the sleeping clergymen of Oxford, who so little honoured their cloth, as he says himself that it was Middleton's unpopularity there which led him to study his writings.

The strange result of this reading was that Gibbon, accepting "the marvellous tales" of the early centuries, was soon ready to embrace "the superior merits of celibacy, the institution of the monastic life, the use of the sign of the cross, of holy oil, and even of images, the invocation of saints, the worship of relics, the rudiments of purgatory in prayers for the dead, and the tremendous mystery of the sacrifice of the body and blood of Christ, which insensibly swelled into the prodigy of transubstantiation". (*Autobiography*, p. 44.)

This last point was indeed crucial. He had listed the other teachings in the style of an historian, implying that he had accepted them, without attraction or repugnance, as parts of the Christian tradition. It would appear that in approaching the doctrine of the Real Presence he had advanced from history into theology, to confront the central mystery of the Christian faith. It is strange and interesting that this was not in fact his approach, even at the time of his conversion; for he faced that mystery too in the spirit of an historian.

The evidence for this is a later passage in his memoirs recording his disavowal of the errors of Popery. What affected him most strongly was this:

> ... the text of Scripture, which seems to inculcate the real presence, is attested only by a single sense—our sight; while the real presence itself is disproved by three of our senses— the sight, the touch, and the taste.
>
> (*Autobiography*, p. 63.)

This remarkable passage makes it clear that he had approached even the Real Presence as an historian, going to the original documents, the Gospels, finding it there stated as a fact, and believing on that evidence.

While this only emphasizes his youth and simplicity at the time of his conversion, it also lessens the astonishment with which some have viewed the change in him, for it reveals that it was a characteristic action, that of the historian. Indeed, just before this passage, he expressly states that it was the study of logic, not history, which led him to disavow his Popery. Yet he returned thereafter to his faith in history and continued to view religion simply as a historical fact, though it is possible to argue that something of the earlier belief was transferred to his respect for Rome. But it is more certain that both his attraction to the Catholic Church and his devotion to the Roman Empire were rooted in the same ground—their history.

This becomes even clearer as he records the next stage in his conversion, when he was lent some books by a man who was up at Magdalen with him. This friend, with whom Gibbon formed "an unlucky intimacy", had some Popish books and opinions, though, unlike Gibbon, he did not act on them. Among these books were a couple of Bossuets, which "achieved my conversion, and I surely fell by a noble hand". One was the *Exposition of the Catholic Doctrine*, the other, the *History of the Protestant Variations*. In this the historical element is stronger, but even in doctrine what impressed Gibbon was the appeal to the first documents of the Church, "the sacramental words, 'Hoc est corpus meum' ".

To this mention of Bossuet, Gibbon's friend Sheffield, who put together his memoirs, adds this note:

> Mr. Gibbon never talked with me on the subject of his conversion to Popery but once: and then, he imputed his change to the works of Parsons, the Jesuit, who lived in the reign of Elizabeth, and who, he said, had urged all the best arguments in favour of the Roman Catholic religion.
>
> (*Autobiography*, p. 47n.)

The work of Parsons, or more correctly Persons, to which this probably refers, is *A Christian Directory Guiding Men to their Eternal Salvation*. There had been numerous editions of this since Elizabethan days, and one of them was even "de-Poped" for the use of Protestants. A Catholic edition had appeared in 1696, and another in London in 1753, the year of Gibbon's conversion. The *Christian Directory* is written in a style which strikes young minds by its appeal to generosity and courage, giving "Divers Reasons, why Tribulations should be received joyfully by us when they come".

To this end, Persons lists "Examples of true resolution", taken from the history of the early Church (of which Gibbon was later to write so differently), to show that "every Catholic that by God's special grace is made worthy to suffer the like in these our days, may take singular comfort and great instruction therein".

To the enquirer who wishes to discover whether he is in the right way, Persons answers, ". . . he that follows universality antiquity, and consent in his belief, and stands firmly to that faith, which has been held in all places, in all seasons . . . may think himself a good Christian".

It was this unity between the early and the later Church which Middleton had already indicated to Gibbon. There was, too, a reference to "Lady Reason", to whom, says Persons, "man by his creation was espoused".

Persons quotes a reference of St. Gregory Nazianzen to the youthful Julian the Apostate, of whom Gibbon was to write with such understanding: "At which time, he says, they foresaw great wickedness in him; notwithstanding, at that time he seemed very devout, and for devotion's sake, though a great prince, he would needs take upon him the office of lector in the Catholic church."

What perhaps strengthened Gibbon's resolution most was Persons' insistence on immediate conversion: "The longer we defer our conversion, the more difficulty we find in it." There was death at hand to emphasize the shortness of time: ". . .neither do thou think that the time will be long, for it flieth and fleeteth with the wind, nor stayeth for any occasion whatsoever." Nor should the Christian be daunted when he remembered the sufferings of past ages: ". . . think not thyself hardly dealt withal, if thou art also called to suffer a little."

Persons was writing for men who had to suffer for their faith. If Bossuet provided the more solid and historical reasons for the conversion, it was perhaps Persons who led Gibbon to act swiftly on them.

There had been changes since Elizabethan days, but legally conversion to Rome still involved the charge of high treason. A convert was also liable to have his property transferred to his nearest relation. The priest receiving him, if no longer in danger of his life, could be sentenced to prison.

Gibbon acted:

> No sooner had I settled my new religion than I resolved to profess myself a Catholic. Youth is sincere and impetuous; and a momentary glow of enthusiasm had raised me above all temporal considerations.
>
> (*Autobiography*, p. 48.)

His father naturally shared neither his enthusiasm nor his aloofness to material prospects. Beyond that, he stood to lose his son and heir, the sole survivor among the seven children whom his wife had borne him, as his property could not pass to a Papist convert. There were other, more immediate effects: "In the first sally of passion he divulged a secret which prudence might have suppressed, and the gates of Magdalen College were for ever shut against my return."

So ended Gibbon's career at Oxford. There, and even in London, the conversion "made some noise", as his friend Sheffield remarks. There was talk of Popish missionaries at work in Oxford, corrupting the youth of the university. Gibbon, in dismissing this outcry of "keen Protestants, who would gladly retaliate the example of persecution", points out that his conversion was entirely a result of his reading and that he never so much as saw a priest or even a Catholic, until he had made his decision, when he applied to a Catholic book-seller in Covent Garden who put him in touch with a priest attached to the Sardinian embassy, the only Catholic centre in London at that time. For doing this he was later summoned before the Privy Council and questioned. The priest, a Jesuit, Father Baker, who had the reputation among his superiors as an "excellent scholar", examined Gibbon and duly received him into the Church: " . . . on the 8th of June, 1753, I solemnly, though privately, adjured the errors of heresy." (*Auto-biography*, p. 49.)

If to Carlyle the church of St. Clement Danes, "where Johnson worshipped in the age of Voltaire", was for ever a holy place, there is perhaps an even stranger solemnity in Gibbon's entry into the Roman communion.

His conversion was the subject of family consultations, at which it was decided to send him, in charge of a Swiss, to Lausanne, where he was to be lodged and tutored by a Cal-vinist minister. He left England only eleven days after his reception into the Church, and eleven days later—a rapid journey at that time—he was in Lausanne.

The father's decision was no less impetuous than that which sent his son to Oxford. Yet, from his own point of view, it was perhaps the wiser of the two. Gibbon was isolated in a strange country where he did not even know the language (for he had less than a schoolboy's French), and he was equally cut off from the sight and affections of home as from his Catholic connections. Nothing remained either of the familiar or of the new delights of his heart.

Even in the ordinary comforts of life the change was abrupt and painful. His expenses had been cut to a minimum, a monthly dole of pocket-money in place of Oxford's boundless credit. He was once more a schoolboy, he who had so seldom endured even the rigours of school:

To a home-bred Englishman every object, every custom was offensive; but the native of any country might have been disgusted with the general aspect of his lodging and entertainment. I had now exchanged an elegant apartment in Magdalen College for a narrow, gloomy street, the most unfrequented of an unhandsome town, for an old inconvenient house, and for a small chamber ill-contrived and ill-furnished, which, on the approach of winter, instead of a companionable fire, must be warmed by the dull, invisible heat of a stove. (*Autobiography*, p. 57.)

In these sad and cheerless circumstances, Gibbon conducted himself with dignity and sense. Few men were less inclined to repine or to bemoan their fate, and he accepted his with the same cheerfulness as he later showed in facing his last illness. He applied himself to learning the French language the more readily because it was necessary to daily life and intercourse. He did this with such success that "before I was recalled home, French, in which I spontaneously thought, was more familiar than English to my ear, my tongue, and my pen". (*Autobiography*, p. 58.)

This was remarkable for a "home-bred Englishman" to whom everything at Lausanne had been "offensive", only less remarkable in view of the fact that he was retained there for nearly five years. He went as a boy of sixteen. It was a man of twenty-one whom his father at last agreed to receive back in England, a delay partly explained by the second marriage which the latter contracted halfway through this period.

In his first years at Lausanne Gibbon's chief consolation was the books in his tutor's library. These were of course in French, which stimulated his efforts to acquire the language, and they were the choice of a Calvinist minister, which was not without its effect on his religious opinions.

This minister, Pavilliard, at once Gibbon's guardian, tutor, and landlord, provided him with the only sustained instruction which he received in childhood, boyhood, or youth. Perhaps the best tribute to his character is contained in the fact that, despite the unfortunate circumstances and cheerless living conditions which were Gibbon's fate on his arrival in Lausanne, he had throughout life a warm affection for the place and later made his own home there, for the majority of men would have been at pains to avoid a district where they had been deprived of everything, both material and spiritual, which had been theirs before. Pavilliard indeed fulfilled the office of a father far better than Gibbon's own.

Gibbon's tribute to him shows more warmth than he displayed in speaking of anybody, only excepting his aunt:

My obligations to the lessons of Mr. Pavilliard, gratitude will not suffer me to forget: he was endowed with a clear head and a warm heart; his innate benevolence had assuaged the spirit of the Church; he was rational, because he was moderate: in the course of his studies he had acquired a just though superficial knowledge of most branches of literature; by long practice, he was skilled in the arts of teaching and he laboured with assiduous patience to know the character, gain the affection, and open the mind of his English pupil. As soon as we began to understand each other, he gently led me, from a blind and undistinguishing love of reading, into the path of instruction.

(*Autobiography*, pp. 59–60.)

It was perhaps the fact that "his innate benevolence had assuaged the spirit of the Church" which operated most strongly on Gibbon, for it was just this absence of zeal, contrasting with the "enthusiasm" of the young convert, which was most apt to impress him. Pavilliard, too, quite apart from his moderation, could hardly have the same abhorrence of Popery as existed in the island of Britain, for Switzerland was surrounded, not by a Protestant sea, but by Catholic lands, and numbered Papists no less than Protestants among its own population. Lausanne was in a Protestant canton, but not in a Protestant country at all comparable to England. Switzerland was just the land to change Gibbon's belief to that of Bayle, who like himself had become a Catholic and then a Protestant, because he "protested against all religions"—Bayle, who "dexterously concludes that custom and education must be the sole grounds of popular belief"—a view which could be conveniently applied to the Catholic and Protestant villages of Switzerland and central Europe, where both followed the religion of their fathers, apart from occasional conversions and intermarriage. Their closeness excluded tolerance, for persecution was still fierce on both sides, but ignorance of Popery was at least less bland than in England, where it sometimes caused a reaction of sympathy towards the Roman Church. It was certainly Pavilliard's moderation in this respect which allowed him to win Gibbon's confidence.

Pavilliard's letters to Gibbon's father show how slowly and discreetly he proceeded. He wrote these letters in French, explaining that his English was not good enough for lengthy conversation, nor was Gibbon's French yet equal to it. Even after Gibbon had been in Lausanne over a month, Pavilliard had still not yet discussed religious questions with him. Two months after Gibbon's arrival Pavilliard reported that he had still not spoken on this, but Gibbon had taken a couple of "controversial books"—presumably religious—to his room. Another two months, and Pavilliard was pleading with Gibbon's father to allow his son more freedom and amusement (the intention had been to confine him to his studies and to the house), for then he would listen to his tutor's arguments with more sympathy. In the same letter Pavilliard noted that Gibbon had Jacobite opinions, to which he had gently opposed his own, apparently with some success. But it was difficult to say whether his ideas had really changed, as he spoke little, and his tutor was anxious not to create the impression that he was trying to win him over.

These Jacobite views reveal not only the persistence of Gibbon's mind, but suggest that he had also been influenced by his Tory ancestors and even by Tory Oxford, where toasts had seldom expressed "the most lively loyalty" to the House of Hanover.

It was just over a year after Gibbon's arrival in Lausanne that Pavilliard was able to report real progress. It had, he wrote to the father, been a long task, as Gibbon was slow to change his ideas. Every point had to be disputed. First Pavilliard had undermined the infallibility of the Church and St. Peter's position as the leader of the Apostles, then the adoration of the Eucharist, then the cult of saints, then purgatory, finally the Lenten fast and Friday abstinence.

It is of interest that this last detail of discipline survived the longest. Pavilliard noticed one Friday that Gibbon was still eating no meat and enquired the reason, fearing that he might be unwell. Gibbon replied that he had refrained deliberately, feeling obliged to conform to the practice of a Church of which he was a member. Pressed, he admitted that he saw no special merit in the custom, but simply thought it a good one. Pavilliard himself regarded it as a small matter, but he admitted that it took him considerable time to "undeceive" his pupil and show him how wrong he was to submit to the discipline of a Church which he no longer regarded as infallible.

Yet perhaps to the young convert it was not so small a matter, as it was the one opportunity he had of asserting his faith in his daily life. The practice was a test of that faith and of his own character, less lurid certainly than that which other ages had imposed, such as that of refusing to spit on the crucifix, but in essence not wholly different. He was quite alone, without any contact with those who shared his faith. This was his last link with them, the last gesture of member-ship in their communion.

Gibbon himself was surprised, he wrote in his memoirs, that the Romish clergy never attempted "to rescue me from the hands of the heretics, or at least to confirm my zeal and constancy in the profession of the faith", when they were in close touch in every part of Europe. But this is to assume a degree of Catholic organization in London of which there is no evidence; nor did Gibbon find any in Oxford. Even if he had been traced to Lausanne, only the most melodramatic intervention could have removed a boy of sixteen from the house of a Calvinist pastor, to whom he had been entrusted by his father.

Yet, in the lack of that outside help, Gibbon would have required not only great strength of character to preserve his faith, but also more wisdom than he had yet acquired, and perhaps a more adventurous spirit than he ever had; for he would have needed to foresee his own failure to resist such an environment, and to escape without money, friends, or know-ledge of the language into a country quite unknown to him.

"The memory of theological opinions cannot long be pre-served" he wrote in Chapter XXVIII of *The Decline and Fall* "without the artificial helps of priests, of temples, and of books." (iii, p. 218.)

The change was to be foreseen, but not by a boy of sixteen in the ardour of his conversion. His defence was "firm and well-managed"—Sheffield appends a note to Gibbon's account of these days in which he says:

55

M. Pavilliard has described to me the astonishment with which he gazed on Mr. Gibbon standing before him: a thin little figure, with a large head, disputing and urging, with the greatest ability, all the best arguments that had ever been used in favour of Popery. Mr. Gibbon many years ago became very fat and corpulent, but he had uncommonly small bones, and was very slightly made.

(*Autobiography*, p. 63*n*.)

"The very best arguments"—it was the same phrase that Sheffield had used of Persons, and it is possible that in Lausanne Gibbon was still drawing on what he had learnt from the Elizabethan Jesuit.

But even Gibbon's "large head" could not prevail in such circumstances, and the "thin little figure" was defeated. Yet while allowing Pavilliard "a handsome share" in the change, he maintained that it was chiefly brought about by his own meditations. It was only natural that he should have some desire to escape from a religion which had caused such disasters in his life, separation from his aunt, the loss of home and family, exile from England, the loss of Oxford, independence and comfort, the narrowness and deprivations of Lausanne, isolation among Calvinists who, however tolerant, regarded it as their first duty to save him from that religion; but he was honest with himself and loyal to his principles— both then and afterwards—requiring solid arguments before he would consent to change his mind. Yet it is evident that when he found them he rejoiced, for he records "his solitary transport" when he came upon the argument against the Real Presence referred to above. His most learned and fair-minded biographer, Mr. D. M. Low, notes here that "in truth it was not philosophy but weariness of what was seen to be nonsense" that caused the change. This scorn for the "nonsense" of Popery has perhaps led him and others to treat Gibbon's conversion with less seriousness than it merits. But it is clear that Gibbon was relieved to free himself from the religion which had overburdened his frail youth: "The various articles of the Romish creed disappeared like a dream; and after a full conviction, on Christmas Day, 1754, I received the sacrament in the church of Lausanne." He was then seventeen and a half, having remained in the Roman communion a little over eighteen months, for nearly the whole of which time he had been stationed in Lausanne.

It is remarkable that in ceasing to be a Papist he had also lost his command of English, for he wrote at once to his aunt in these odd phrases: "I have at length good news to tell you. I am now good Protestant, and am extremely glad of it." At the end of the letter he wrote of feeling "a joy extremely pure", an obviously French construction. Already, after only eighteen months, he was less proficient in English than in French, in which language he was to write his first work.

What his religious opinions were after this experience is less easy to affirm. Of the decisive moment in Lausanne at Christmas, 1754, he later wrote: "It was here that I suspended my religious enquiries, acquiescing with implicit belief in the tenets and mysteries which are adopted by the general consent of Catholics and Protestants." (*Autobiography*, p. 63.) It is a broad statement, and acquiescence has scarcely the force of belief. He remained a sincere Protestant in Lausanne, and it is uncertain when he changed into the sceptic or deist apparent in *The Decline and Fall*, where he distinguished so little between religions, speaking indifferently, for instance, in Chapter XLVII, of "the prejudices of a Papist or a Protestant" (v, p. 162), and showing indulgence to none, unless it was to the Mohammedans, for in Chapter L he wrote: "A philosophic Atheist might subscribe the popular creed of the Mohammedans:

a creed too sublime perhaps for our present faculties." (v, p. 362.) Yet some such creed was perhaps eventually Gibbon's own.

Cotter Morison believed that he remained a Protestant up to 1763, when he was twenty-six, but there are grounds for believing that the change came earlier. Thereafter his indifference increased. As late as 1788, only six years before his death, he wrote to his aunt Hester: "I can assure you with truth that I consider Religion as the best guide of youth and the best support of old age." But that omitted the years of maturity and was obviously prompted by indulgence—Mr. Low wisely points out that a man is not on oath to his aunt. Even so, Gibbon was careful not to say that he himself believed in religion. But in the following year the French Revolution began to strengthen in him this opinion that it was a good thing for others, and his mind altered in a way somewhat similar to that of Bolivar, who had shared the "enlightened" philosophy of Gibbon, but thought more kindly of the Church in his last years, as a politician, not as a philosopher.

Certainly it was as a philosopher that Gibbon died, after long years of antipathy for those religious debates which had so disrupted his youth.

V

THE LOVER'S SIGH

... she listened to the voice of truth and passion, and I might presume to hope that I had made some impression on a virtuous heart. At Crassy and Lausanne I indulged my dream of felicity: but on my return to England, I soon discovered that my father would not hear of this strange alliance, and that without his consent I was myself destitute and helpless. After a painful struggle I yielded to my fate: I sighed as a lover, I obeyed as a son; my wound was insensibly healed by time, absence, and the habits of a new life.   (*Autobiography*, pp. 83–4.)

GIBBON'S five years' exile in Lausanne became pleasanter once he had acquired French and was again a good Protestant. Restrictions were relaxed and he saw some English company, among whom he contracted a gambling debt which so upset him that he made a wild escapade to Geneva, from where he was brought back by the discreet and understanding Pavilliard. It has been suggested that he showed more spirit in this escapade than in his conversion; it is also to the point that he had a horse, supplied by his gaming companion, and more knowledge of the country and the language. After this episode, he relied more on French company.

He was in fact becoming increasingly French. When he wrote to his aunt, French constructions appeared on the paper as he gave her "this plain recite of my situation". To his father he even wrote a letter in French and expressed his dismay with a reply which showed "Dear Edward *changé en un froid*

Monsieur". His father's remarriage was not calculated to heal the breach with his son, and it was not until Gibbon returned to England that he found how different his stepmother was from the legends of that relation.

Writing to his aunt, he said, took him a whole day, because he was obliged to write in English: "This last reason will seem a paradox, but I assure you the French is much more familiar to me." Yet that was in September 1755, when he had been in Lausanne a few months over two years.

In his memoirs he noted that one result of his Swiss education was that "I had ceased to be an Englishman. At the flexible period of youth, from the age of sixteen to twenty-one, my opinions, habits, and sentiments were cast in a foreign mould; the faint and distant remembrance of England was almost obliterated; my native language was grown less familiar; and I should have cheerfully accepted the offer of a moderate independence on the terms of perpetual exile." (*Autobiography*, p. 85.)

One of the reasons which led him to contemplate exile so cheerfully was that he had already found love and friendship in it.

It was among the Swiss of Lausanne that Gibbon formed his first real friendship, with a young man of his own age, Deyverdun. They met again later in England, and finally shared the house in Lausanne where *The Decline and Fall* was completed. This first period in Lausanne was the only settled and healthy period which fate had yet presented to Gibbon, and it is significant of its permanent influence on him that it should also have offered him his first friend.

It also gave him his first and only love, for it was with Deyverdun that he met Suzanne Curchod, the daughter of a minister in Crassy, in the mountains between Vaud and Burgundy. When she visited relations in Lausanne, she was generally admired, not only for her charms, but for her virtues and her vivacious intelligence. Her father had given her the education which had been more usually reserved for males, and she was herself to become the mother of Madame de Staël, whose writings had such influence on the French Romantics.

Suzanne Curchod, whose own mother had been French, appears to have created in Lausanne something of the stir which so often accompanies Frenchwomen among people less experienced in the arts of pleasing. She shone, she was brilliant—the sort of girl for whom a brilliant future is also prophesied. It has been suggested that she had another quality which is sometimes associated with Frenchwomen—a swift ability to guard and further her own material interests. Perhaps this quality had a place in her, but it is not one opposed to sincere and even romantic affection. She was one of those women whose dearest dream is to fall in love with an out-standing man, and who are therefore more inclined to admire a man for what he will be, or for what they will make of him, than for what he is. Such characters may not be ambitious in the material sense, for in their realism they are often aware that life with a gifted man involves many sacrifices, but they are sometimes calculating and have an eye for the future which to others may seem more worldly than it really is. It is a fine point, but an important one, as critics have not on the whole been kind to Suzanne Curchod, nor to Gibbon in this affair; for both of them had the same sort of prudence, in that they had a reasonable regard for the future. But it is too much to say, simply because Lausanne was not Verona and they were not Romeo and Juliet, that there was not real love and even passion between them. Suicide is not, after all, the only or even the highest test of love.

It is certain that Gibbon was immediately bewitched by Suzanne Curchod. In his *Journal* for June 1757, he noted:

"I saw Mademoiselle Curchod—*Omnia vincit amor, et nos cedamus amori*"—nor is there any reason to doubt that he was then sure that love would indeed conquer everything, as sure as he had been that his father would become reconciled to his conversion to Popery. It was not that there was any religious difference, for Suzanne too was a good Protestant, even the daughter of a minister.

In a letter probably written in this year, Gibbon declared after a parting that Adam chased from Paradise was luckier than himself. The lovers corresponded, but it would be idle to look for the romanticism of a later generation either in the elegance of Gibbon or in the modesty of Suzanne, nor had either of them the temperament to keep letters in which too much had been revealed. But he confessed that he had read one of her letters forty-two times.

In his memoirs Gibbon was circumspect: "I hesitate from the apprehension of ridicule, when I approach the delicate subject of my early love." Yet on the next page he forthrightly admitted: "I saw and loved. I found her learned without pedantry, lively in conversation, pure in sentiment, and elegant in manners; and the first sudden emotion was fortified by the habits and knowledge of a more familiar acquaintance." (*Autobiography*, p. 83.) In November 1757, he stayed for six days at Crassy, the home of the Curchods.

She was as pleased with him, and perhaps for similar reasons, as they had much in common. Both had vivacity, and both had distinction. So staid an authority as the *Cambridge History of English Literature* has noted Gibbon's "inexhaustive vivacity of mind", which throughout his life always made him attractive company for women. If his looks were unequal to the charm of Suzanne, he had the distinction which had more effect on a woman as intelligent as herself. He was also a foreigner, an Englishman, in the great age of England, which was, further, exercising a strong intellectual influence on the Continent. They could both enjoy the contrast of nationality, so often a charm to young lovers, without the barrier of language, as Gibbon was already more proficient in French than in English; but beyond this they shared the warm friendship and common interests which are among the best preservatives of love.

It was the difference of nationality to which Gibbon's father objected, though this might have been less forbidding if Suzanne had had a dowry to cross the sea with her. Even the ban on the lovers did not destroy the natural friendship between them, which survived until their deaths—both died in the same year.

Gibbon's resistance to his father's decree might have been stronger if he had not already submitted once, in the matter of his conversion, and if he had not devoted the whole of his five years' stay in Lausanne to trying to win his way back into his father's favour. It had been a long process, in which he had exercised much tact and much obedience, and he only became a lover when he had devoted the whole of his energies to the duties of a son, so that his famous antithesis, which has occasioned so much unconsidered amusement, between the sighs of the lover and the obedience of the son, candidly confessed a very real dilemma. A young man who had just given up nearly five years of his life to doing his father's will and had at last succeeded, was not in the strongest position to challenge it again.

It was in the spring of 1758 that his father at last agreed to his return home. This was during the Seven Years' War between Britain and France, which was fought all over the globe. The French were so "peevish and difficult" as to refuse a passage to English travellers. In consequence Gibbon travelled with an assumed name and uniform in the company of two Swiss officers in the service of the Dutch.

Back in London, he hurried to Westminster to the house of his aunt, "the only person in England whom I was impatient to see". Yet the homecoming to his father's house was attended with none of the distress in which he had departed from it. His father received him "as a man and a friend", and before long he found that the stepmother of whom he had been so apprehensive was not only a charming woman, but indulgently disposed towards him, with the result that, "as Mrs. Gibbon had neither children nor the hopes of children, we more easily adopted the tender names and genuine characters of mother and of son". (*Autobiography*, p. 88.)

This welcome he received from father and stepmother weakened his resistance on the one point of conflict: his father would not hear of the "strange alliance" with Suzanne Curchod, to whom Gibbon had written, shortly after leaving Lausanne, that he knew "the joy of the Martyrs" on being separated from her. After his father's ultimatum he wrote to tell her that he had retired to his room for two hours, then gone to his father to say that he would sacrifice his life's happiness to him. She was hurt that it had taken him so short an interval to decide.

On Gibbon's behalf it may be recalled that in the *Arabian Nights*, which had been the favourite book of his childhood, occurs the observation that "blood has no less power than love on noble souls".

Mr. Peter Quennell, in his study of Gibbon in *Four Portraits*, has doubted whether the struggle to renounce Suzanne was "painful", and it is true that he had resisted longer on the question of his religion, though the pressure exercised then was both greater and far more prolonged; but it was inevitable that, having given way on that, and having gained the benefit of so happy a return home, he should be the less able to assert himself in his second struggle. Nor was this surrender only a selfish one for his own security, as he had nothing to offer Suzanne if his father withheld support. His education at Lausanne had already drawn him to the life of a scholar, but he had no university, nor office, nor patron, nor were either he or Suzanne likely inhabita.ts of garrets or Grub Street. If he was bowing to reason and prudence in accepting his father's decision, it was in consideration of her future no less than of his own.

There has been a tendency among critics of Gibbon to dismiss both his conversion and his love affair as boyish peccadillos, odd or amusing, which had little or no effect on the character of the mature man. Yet most men are recognizably themselves between sixteen and twenty, and some would put the formative period much earlier. Nor is the fact that Gibbon was later sceptical both about religion and about women a valid argument that he had no experience or understanding of them, for it frequently happens that a shock in youth decides an attitude for life, as cynicism often masks a wounded sensibility.

Some who have wished to defend Christianity against him have argued that he had no religious sensibility, while others, concerned to defend a later ideal of romantic love, have argued that he had a cold temperament incapable of a deep attachment. Such judgments on the inner substance of a man's spirit are rarely more than approximate, but it is interesting that they are the two criticisms most commonly levelled against Gibbon, while his conversion and his love affair are the two events in his life most commonly dismissed with amusement or indifference.

Porson's malicious and often quoted remark, "Nor does his humanity ever slumber unless when women are ravished or the Christians persecuted", brings the two criticisms together. It is a wise remark. Gibbon was humane, but his French outlook made him less than English in the style of his moral indignation. It is striking that, when it is a question of women and Christians, there is an absence of that warmth which inspires his pages when he treats of Rome, of a great man, or of a great occasion—in its place, a coldness punctuated by irony.

This is often enough the tone of a man who has suffered and has resolved to avoid those things or people responsible for his pain. Gibbon had had experience both of religion and of love, and both experiences had been painful. In both he had failed to achieve either the future or the character he had planned for himself. It was only natural that he should not trust himself again, particularly not in those sorts of experience which had caused him suffering.

The connection between religion and love, both in the experience of his youth and in the tone in which he later wrote of them, indicates the grounds of his scepticism. His doubts were centred less on them than on human motives, in which there is an obvious difference between him and a whole-hearted sceptic such as Hume, whose tone remains the same, good-natured and level, whatever his subject. But Gibbon's doubts are strongest when he considers religion and love. He had good grounds for his doubts, as his own experience had proved their failure to resist the pressure of circumstance. In this too perhaps is to be found the explanation of the constant balancing of motives which is so typical of his writing (see Chapter X below).

He was the less able to resist his father's decrees because he had known so little security in his own life, ill, unsettled, or exiled. He could only make himself comfortable by doubting his own motives, to reach the serene conviction that he was not really a Papist, that he was not really in love with Suzanne.

In his conversion, the pressure against him had been

overwhelming, but it was less strong in his love affair, however peremptory was his father's decree. It was less strong,
but Gibbon himself was also weaker. He was no longer alone,
for he had the loyalty and the affection of Suzanne to support
him. He had friends in Switzerland. Yet he yielded. Indulgence may urge that he was considering her future, but Suzanne
did not want that consideration; like other women in her
case, she wanted constancy in her lover. Gibbon, like other
men in his case, laid himself open to the charges of weakness,
heartlessness, and self-interest.

A reading of the letters that passed between them afterwards
creates something of the disagreeable impression in the
correspondence between Eloise and Abelard. The woman
shows so much more nobility than the man. But the tragic
point in that was that Abelard had been so brutally deprived
of his manhood by his enemies. Some may feel that in this
affair Gibbon, without the same excuse, displayed less than the
character of a man. Nor can he be said to have made himself a
eunuch for the kingdom of heaven's sake, for it was his future
in the urbane salons of the eighteenth century that was at stake,
his snuff-box, his elegant coats, his comfort.

The impression would be less disagreeable if it could be
shown that Suzanne was as worldly in her outlook as himself.
The brilliant marriage which she later made might be used as
evidence of this, but that can hardly reveal her behaviour in
an earlier affair, and that behaviour, unfortunately, reveals no
lack either of dignity or of affection. It is true that she persisted, but that appears to have been because, apart from
announcing his father's judgment, Gibbon gave her no clear
indication of the feelings in his own heart.

His subsequent references to her—"the Curchod"—have
the negligent tone of a man of the world who has successfully
escaped from the clutches of a woman, marred only by the

consciousness that she has since made a more splendid conquest. This worldly tone, which became normal to him in his references to women, both in his private and in his public writings, is sometimes assumed to echo the voice of experience, but may more often convey a lack of experience in, or a flight from, the deeper emotions. In the grave and judicious pages of *The Decline and Fall*, Gibbon's references to women have at times the self-conscious audacity exhibited by schoolboys—by whom they are most keenly relished.

In the irony with which Gibbon treats the deeper passions, whether these are aroused by divine or by human love, there is an amusement which ends by becoming tedious, like the frisking of a dog. Yet it is a tribute to his social graces that women, for whom irony is usually an unpleasing male grimace, enjoyed his company. He was on excellent terms with his friends' wives, more to the relief than to the anxiety of their husbands. Perhaps both felt secure in his lack of seriousness, in his absence of passion. After his one affair, his tone consistently became lighter.

Yet Suzanne, who had not been through the experience of an earlier surrender to parental authority, could not adapt herself so easily. She persisted, until letters were intercepted and finally there was silence between the lovers.

But this was not destined to end the association between them. Five years later, at the age of twenty-six, Gibbon was at last able to embark on the Grand Tour, passing some months in Paris in the spring of 1763, then nearly a year in Lausanne before going on to Rome.

Soon after his arrival in Lausanne, she wrote to him asking for "a complete avowal of his indifference". She also offered to give him an introduction to Rousseau, who had been acquainted with the affair. This manœuvre has drawn criticism on Suzanne as an intriguer, but such plots, not unknown in these affairs, are far from disproving the sincerity of love. Anyhow, this introduction, even if Gibbon had accepted it—which he did not—would hardly have furthered her cause, as is clear from Rousseau's own words on the affair:

> He who does not appreciate Mdlle Curchod is not worthy of her; he who appreciates her and separates himself from her is a man to be despised. She does not know what she wants. Gibbon serves her better than her own heart. I would rather a hundred times that he left her poor and free among you than that he should take her off to be rich and miserable in England.

Gibbon himself supplied the reference to this passage in his memoirs, adding:

> As an author I shall not appeal from the judgment, or taste, or caprice of *Jean Jacques*; but that extraordinary man, whom I admire and pity, should have been less precipitate in condemning the moral character and conduct of a stranger.
> (*Autobiography*, p. 84*n*.)

In June 1763, Gibbon, embarrassed by her persistence, wrote to Suzanne: "Must you always offer me a happiness which reason forces me to renounce?"

In September, finally resigned, she wrote to him: "One day you will regret your irreparable loss."

But he was making progress in his indifference, for in the same year he was able to observe that "this affair, in all respects so strange, has been very useful to me". It would, he said, be "a safeguard against the seductions of love".

Then again there was silence, but while Gibbon pursued his Grand Tour, Suzanne went as a companion to Paris, where she met the rich Swiss banker, Necker, and was installed there as his wife when Gibbon returned through Paris in 1765.

In a letter to Holroyd, later Lord Sheffield, whose friendship he had made on his second stay in Lausanne, he described their meeting:

> The Curchod (Madame Necker) I saw at Paris. She was very fond of me, and the husband particularly civil. Could they insult me more cruelly? Ask me every evening to supper; go to bed and leave me alone with his wife—what an impertinent security! It is making an old lover of mighty little consequence. She is as handsome as ever, and much genteeler; seems pleased with her fortune rather than proud of it. I was (perhaps indiscreetly enough) exalting Nanette de Illens's good luck and the fortune. "What fortune?" said she with an air of contempt, "not above 20,000 livres a year." I smiled, and she caught herself immediately. "What airs I give myself in despising 20,000 livres a year, who a year ago looked upon 800 as the summit of my wishes.

The tone of the bachelor is already there, and perhaps of something else. Mr. Michael Joyce, in the most recent study of Gibbon, has written: "There was something of the male flirt about Gibbon, now that his one true passion was behind him." That was indeed the sort of bachelor he became, yet his friendships with women were genuine enough, and that with Suzanne persisted so long that he may almost have found in her that "affection perhaps softened by the secret influence of sex, but pure from any mixture of sensual desire", which he had missed in a sister.

Suzanne herself wrote of this meeting in Paris to a friend:

> I have seen Gibbon, and it has given me more pleasure than I know how to express. Not indeed that I retain my

sentiment for a man who I think does not deserve much; but my feminine vanity could not have had a more complete and honest triumph. He stayed two weeks in Paris, and I had him every day at my house; he has become soft, yielding, humble, decorous to a fault. He was a constant witness of my husband's kindness, wit, and gaiety, and made me remark for the first time, by his admiration for wealth, the opulence with which I am surrounded, and which up to this moment had only produced a disagreeable impression upon me.

This aftermath perhaps does injustice to both of them, as both were glossing over the passion of the past with present satisfactions. Yet both were ambitious and could admire the achievements of ambition in the other. She later rejoiced with the triumphant historian of the Roman Empire, while he, in closing the brief account of his love affair in his memoirs, could dwell on her later triumphs—"and Mademoiselle Curchod is now the wife of M. Necker, the minister, and perhaps the legislator, of the French monarchy."

It can seldom have happened that a man and a woman, both so resolved to conquer circumstances and rise to the position that their gifts and characters designed for them, should have loved and parted and realized their ambitions—she as the wife of a French minister, he as the most illustrious of English historians—and remained friends for life. Yet it is possible that it was just this distinction, this sense of a destiny above their existing circumstances, which first drew them together. It is even more likely that they would not have remained friends if either had fallen by the wayside. It was their practical sense in ordering their own lives which both separated them and made them successful, later to bring them together as friends. Such sacrifices of love to careers occur often enough, but rarely with such happy results, though happier perhaps for Suzanne than for Gibbon, as she only lost one husband, while in her he lost the only woman he might have married (as he could hardly find another with her qualities). Ten years after this meeting in Paris he wrote to her that English-women were "eternal ice"; and those who were attractive were sadly lacking in education compared with Suzanne.

In 1767, when he was thirty, he had already written to Holroyd as a confirmed bachelor: ". . . tho' as a philosopher I may prefer celibacy yet as a politician I think it highly proper that the species should be propagated by the usual method."

By that time he was also confirmed in the character of a sceptic, one who employed the same bantering tone in talking of women and religion, sometimes joining the two, as in Chapter LVIII of *The Decline and Fall*, where he was to write of the medieval knight: "As the champion of God and the ladies (I blush to unite such discordant names), he devoted himself to speak the truth . . ." (vi, p. 293.) The same tone and theme occurs in a letter he wrote in 1775: "Yet you refuse me the qualities of a valiant knight always ready to break a lance in the honour of God and the Ladies."

This was the Gibbon who, when writing his most learned Chapter XLIV on Roman Jurisprudence, which was later adopted as a treatise for use in European universities, pointed out that "the liberty of divorce does not contribute to happiness and virtue. The facility of separation would destroy all mutual confidence, and inflame every trifling dispute: the minute difference between a husband and a stranger, which might so easily be removed, might still more easily be forgotten; and the matron, who in five years can submit to the embrace of eight husbands, must cease to reverence the chastity of her own person". (iv, p. 510.) Then he added a footnote: "Jerome saw at Rome a triumphant husband bury his twenty-first wife, who had interred twenty-two of his less sturdy predecessors. But the ten husbands in a month of the poet Martial is an extravagant hyperbole."

The same gaiety of tone marked his references to women in his letters. When in 1777 his stepmother raised objections to his going to Paris, he answered by ridiculing her two fears, first, "that I shall be confined or put to death by the priests", second, "that I shall sully my *moral* character by making love to Necker's wife". On this he added: "The constancy and danger of a twenty years' passion is a subject upon which I hardly know how to be serious." Yet later in the same year he was writing to Suzanne, Necker's wife, that "our souls know how to speak without using pen or post", a gallant excuse for dilatoriness in correspondence. He also referred to her friendship as "the consolation and the glory" of his life. Three years later another letter assured her that "I will never forget the dearest days of my youth".

Yet even in his gallantry he was rarely insincere, and it is easy to believe, from such remarks, that something remained of his youthful passion, even if he "hardly knew how to be serious" about it. At least there was no other woman, just as a few years after his Popery there was no other religion: Lausanne had seen the best of his faith and his love, and it was fitting that he should eventually settle down there to finish his life's work.

If, even when fat and elderly, he remained gallant towards women, there was never any question of a serious attachment. An anecdote due to the malice of Mme de Genlis credits him with going down on his knees to make a proposal and then being unable to rise owing to his corpulence. It was doubtless the contrast between gallantry and corpulence which gave rise to the various versions of this fictitious incident.

Friends were ready enough to find wives for him, even when he was nearer fifty than forty, but he showed his reluctance in a letter to Lady Sheffield written in 1784:

I have discovered about half a dozen *Wives* who would please me in different ways and by various merits: one as a Mistress . . . a second, a lively entertaining acquaintance, a third a sincere good-natured friend, a fourth who would represent with grace and dignity at the head of my table and family, a fifth an excellent economist and housekeeper, and a sixth a very useful nurse. (Letter of 22 Oct. 1784.)

When he was safely over fifty, the reluctance became more marked: "Were I ten years younger I might possibly think of a female companion, but the choice is difficult, the success doubtful, the engagement perpetual . . ."

So it was that some months after his death Maria Josepha Holroyd could note that of Suzanne in the same year with the words: "Madame Necker had the satisfaction of going out of the world with the knowledge of being Mr. Gibbon's First and Only Love."

VI

THE GREAT REPUBLIC

It is the duty of a patriot to prefer and promote the exclusive interest and glory of his native country: but a philosopher may be permitted to enlarge his views, and to consider Europe as one great republic, whose various inhabitants have attained almost the same level of politeness and cultivation. The balance of power will continue to fluctuate, and the prosperity of our own, or the neighbouring kingdoms, may be alternately exalted or depressed; but these partial events cannot essentially injure our general state of happiness, the system of arts, and laws, and manners, which so advantageously distinguish, above the rest of mankind, the Europeans and their colonies.

(Gibbon, "General Observations on the Fall of the Roman Empire in the West," *The Decline and Fall*, ch. xxxviii (vol. iv, p. 176).)]

IN pursuing the affair of Suzanne Curchod and the subsequent history of Gibbon's sentiments, "the doubtful arrangement of dates" has been rejected in favour of "the more natural distribution of subjects". The years that elapsed between his return from Lausanne in 1758, when he was twenty-one, to his departure for Paris and the Grand Tour at the beginning of 1763, were passed at his father's house at Buriton, near Petersfield in Hampshire, less than sixty miles from London, where he also stayed for nine months, and in the Hampshire militia.

In London, he "assiduously frequented the theatre at a

very propitious era of the stage, when a constellation of excellent actors, both in tragedy and comedy, was eclipsed by the meridian brightness of Garrick in the maturity of his judgement and vigour of his performance". But he was himself not yet ripe for that social life which he was later to enjoy:

> I had not been endowed by art or nature with those happy gifts of confidence and address, which unlock every door and every bosom; nor would it be reasonable to complain of the just consequences of my sickly childhood, foreign education, and reserved temper. While coaches were rattling through Bond Street, I have passed many a solitary evening in my lodging with my books. My studies were sometimes interrupted by a sigh, which I breathed towards Lausanne . . .
>
> (*Autobiography*, p. 90.)

It was typical of him that he considered it unreasonable to complain. He had accepted his fate, yet this "sigh towards Lausanne" reveals that he was more deeply moved than might appear from that other sigh with which he had obeyed his father.

He was less happy in the country than in town, for he never adapted himself to country pursuits: "I never handled a gun, I seldom mounted a horse; and my philosophic walks were soon terminated by a shady bench, where I was long detained by the sedentary amusement of reading or meditation."

He was as little adapted to the round of country dinners and visits, and he "dreaded the period of the full moon, which was usually reserved for our more distant excursions".

From these activities he escaped as often as he could to his reading, and had already begun to form his own library: "I cannot forget the joy with which I exchanged a banknote of twenty pounds for the twenty volumes of the *Memoirs of the Academy of Inscriptions*." His love of reading had brought him to agree with the elder Pliny—and with Don Quixote—that no book was so bad as not to have some good in it. But it was perhaps not only as a scholar that he followed the lessons in a Greek Testament on Sundays; there was still some religion left in him, and his scepticism developed further only on his return to the Continent for the Grand Tour.

In this development of his opinions, there were in England other influences at work, though these too were of French origin and had already affected him while he was still living in Lausanne. Gibbon's notes on his reading show references to the volumes of Bayle and Le Clerc, who both cast their teaching in an encyclopaedic mould and created a Protestant Enlightenment well in advance of the more famous movement in metropolitan France.

Bayle, who was ten years older than Le Clerc, had been born in southern France—in the Ariège, just north of the Pyrenees—in the middle of the seventeenth century. His family was Calvinist, but local pressures and the thirst for knowledge sent him to be educated—and converted—by the Jesuits at Toulouse. Afterwards, he returned to Protestantism, because, in his famous phrase already quoted, he "protested against all religions", and settled in Rotterdam, where in 1697 he produced his great *Historical and Critical Dictionary* and established his reputation as an enlightened French critic.

That Gibbon was keenly aware of the parallel between his own and Bayle's conversion is shown by the couple of pages which he devotes to him in his *Autobiography* (pp. 51–3), speaking of him with evident admiration. Later (p. 77) he wrote to his aunt suggesting that he might study at a University in Holland, and on his return to England he "stepped aside" to visit Rotterdam. Bayle had then been dead for over half a century, but it is possible that the visit was prompted by piety towards one whom he regarded as a master.

It was Bayle who set the fashion, in his *News of the Republic of Letters* in 1684, and in his *Dictionary*, for discursive works of criticism which anticipated the Encyclopaedia of Diderot and D'Alembert. As a compiler, though perhaps not as a critic, he was surpassed by Le Clerc, who had no great opinion of his learning. Le Clerc, born of a Calvinist family in Geneva, also retired to the more congenial and more tolerant climate of Holland, where he settled in Amsterdam and produced his *Universal and Historical Library* and his *Selected Library*, which Gibbon considered the more brilliant work. He was a pioneer in the field of modern biblical criticism, and it is probable that it was from him that Gibbon learnt the critical methods which he applied to early Christian texts.

The work of both Bayle and Le Clerc was known in England —Le Clerc in 1682 had preached in the Savoy Chapel. The Enlightenment even had disciples there, among them David Mallet, a Scot (his name was originally Malloch), who had some reputation as a poet and dramatist, being a close friend of Garrick. His second wife, daughter of the Earl of Carlisle's steward, brought Mallet ten thousand pounds, and he had settled in a house in Putney, where he became an intimate friend of Gibbon's father, who was an old Putney resident.

On Gibbon's conversion at Oxford, his father had carried him off to the Mallets' house, where, Gibbon noted in his *Autobiography* (p. 56), he was "rather scandalised than reclaimed" by Mallet's philosophy. Gibbon senior evidently had some traits of the Tory squire who, whether shocked or amused by the antics of intellectuals, keeps one among his friends to consult in a crisis of ideas, as he would consult a surgeon in a severe attack of gout. To his simplicity it might well have appeared that Mallet's freethinking—he had the reputation of "a great declaimer in all the London coffee-houses against Christianity"—was the best antidote to his son's Popery.

When that son returned to England, cured, Gibbon senior again introduced him into the Mallet household, perhaps to guard against a relapse. Whatever were the father's own opinions (and there is nothing to indicate that they were not those of a conventional Tory squire), he could be reassured by the wealth that had come to Mallet with his second wife, the more as he was so incompetent in managing his own finances. He may even have acquired some tincture of Mallet's opinions, but it is more certain that he would have preferred his son to share those, to which no social or political disabilities were attached, than to fall back into Popery. There was probably no danger of that, but the father had only recently renewed contact with his son, after an absence of five years, and had no means of judging whether the cure was permanent. The Mallets would be a wholesome influence, as they were not only secure from Popery, but even from Christianity. Anyhow, David Mallet was a man of intellectual interests, and it was already clear, even to the sight of a not very understanding father, that the younger Gibbon shared these, making it natural that he should also discuss them with the older man.

Gibbon himself in his *Autobiography* (p. 90) noted: "The most useful friends of my father were the Mallets: they received me with civility and kindness at first on his account, and afterwards on my own." Soon he was *"domesticated"* with them, finding a young man's satisfaction in having his enlarged views further extended by a mature critic, while Mallet himself enjoyed the pleasure of impressing his opinions on a willing follower and forming a mind of much greater range than his own.

Gibbon's own estimate of Mallet remained high even when, many years later, he came to write his memoirs, though with other writers, among them Voltaire, he added a rider to say that in his youth he had rated them above their real merit:

> Mr. Mallet, a name among the English poets, is praised by an unforgiving enemy, for the ease and elegance of his conversation, and his wife was not destitute of wit or learning.

This reference (p. 90) is a marked contrast to Lord Sheffield's note (p. 56):

> The author of a *Life of Bacon*, which has been rated above its value; of some forgotten poems and plays; and of the pathetic ballad of William and Margaret. His tenets were deistical; perhaps a stronger term might have been used.

Possibly Mallet was the original inspiration of Gibbon's deism, that uncertain philosophy which, while it would speak with piety or platitude of the "Author of Nature", as often copied the traits of atheism in its contempt for any metaphysic or religion more clearly defined than its own. It resembled nineteenth-century agnosticism in discarding all religious concepts except the capital letters with which it garnished its more splendid phrases. But it is evident that in its early days it induced a feeling of liberation, as if in rejecting the traditional gods and beliefs of mankind it had really cleared an immense space between earth and sky, in which the human spirit could soar to new heights. Perhaps the nearest modern analogy to it is the invention of aircraft, or the hope of penetrating to Mars, or at least the moon.

It is not difficult for contemporary philosophers to dismiss such flights as abuses of language, only less absurd than the misuse of capital letters; but it is important to realize that they were inspired by deep emotions. To the eighteenth century they were particularly congenial, because the elevation provided by looking down on the traditional beliefs of mankind was in accord with the aristocratic cast of its thought. It might be possible to argue that all great atheists and many agnostics are in essence aristocrats, riding high above the common people and common religions of mankind, sometimes dreaming, as Nietzsche, of producing a race of such supermen. Gibbon never achieved that lonely eminence, but he was climbing the path to it, for he equated scepticism with an aristocratic intelligence, as is clear from a reference in *The Decline and Fall* (ii, p. 59) to its being confined to "a few inquisitive minds".

It is also possible that the breathing of this more rarefied air sent Gibbon back with stronger respect for the busts and medals, the more solid monuments of imperial Rome, to find in the buildings raised to the gods that deeper emotion which the majority of men had found in the gods themselves. As a deist he could despise the ideas of the past, but he did not make the mistake, fatal to a historian, of despising the men who had held them, however much greater his sympathy for a sceptical emperor than for one who was a believer.

It was David Mallet who set him on the way to deism, but it was also Mallet who prompted the style which was to celebrate Rome:

By the judicious advice of Mr. Mallet, I was directed to the writings of Swift and Addison; wit and simplicity are their common attributes: but the style of Swift is supported by manly original vigour; that of Addison is adorned by the female graces of elegance and mildness.

(*Autobiography*, p. 95.)

81

Mallet's advice was indeed judicious, as these manly and female elements are mixed in the style of Gibbon, as they were perhaps in his own nature (for this might explain the alternation of his pleasure in the company of women and his withdrawal from them).

Another important result of Gibbon's friendship with Mallet was the strengthening of those influences from the Protestant Enlightenment in the Low Countries which he had already acquired from the reading of Le Clerc and Bayle. It was not only that he returned to this reading, as is shown by a note in the *Journal* for 29 August 1761:

> However, having finished Voltaire, I returned to Le Clerc (I mean for the amusement of my leisure hours); and laid aside for some time his *Bibliothèque Universelle* to look into the *Bibliothèque Choisie*, which is by far the better work.

Not only that, but Mallet introduced him to Dr. Maty, an upholder of the same opinions, with an official position at the British Museum, who gave his attention to Gibbon's first printed work:

> A writer can seldom be content with the doubtful recompense of solitary approbation; but a youth ignorant of the world, and of himself, must desire to weigh his talents in some scales less partial than his own: my conduct was natural, my motive laudable, my choice of Dr. Maty judicious and fortunate. By descent and education, Dr. Maty, though born in Holland, might be considered as a Frenchman; but he was fixed in London by the practice of physic, and an office in the British Museum. His reputation was justly founded on the eighteen volumes of the *Journal Britannique*, which he had supported, almost alone, with perseverance

and success. This humble though useful labour, which had once been dignified by the genius of Bayle and the learning of Le Clerc, was not disgraced by the taste, the knowledge, and the judgement of Maty... (*Autobiography*, p. 96.)

It was a labour of this sort which was later, for an interval, to occupy Gibbon on his return from the Grand Tour, when he was impelled to play his part in the Enlightenment. But the work which he submitted to Maty was one which he had already begun to write in French when he was still at Lausanne, an *Essay on the Study of Literature*. He pursued it in the same language, partly for that reason and because French was natural to him—even six years after the *Essay* he said in a letter to Hume: "I write in French, because I think in French"—and partly because, as he himself confessed, he had a vanity to write in the "common dialect" of European civilization, as French then was. Though the Seven Years' War was still in progress, that was far from interrupting this civilized tradition: it was even a convenience, as Gibbon had the manuscript transcribed by one of the French prisoners at Petersfield.

The *Essay* was mainly concerned in the battle between the "Ancients" and the "Moderns", then a favourite topic with French men of letters—the question whether there was more merit and interest in a study of Greek and Roman writers or in those of the more modern, one revived more recently in the form of debates on the value of a classical education. Gibbon had naturally set himself to defend the ancients. "A knowledge of antiquity" he wrote "is our best commentary."

The *Essay* is written in rhetorical and "brilliant" French, such as so often tempts young Englishmen who have conceived an admiration for these qualities in the language, without those of sobriety and judgment with which the French themselves know how to balance them. But it is a considerable achievement, and it is Gibbon himself who makes the best criticism of it, that "if we except some introductory pages, all the remaining chapters might indifferently be reversed or transposed". These very brief "chapters" are indeed more in the nature of aphorisms, betraying both the short wind and the desire for brilliance of a young man. The long stride of the Gibbon period was still to come, but the *Essay* occasionally has the pregnancy of his briefer sentences.

The last words of the *Essay*, "The good of the art is much dearer to me than the glory of the artist", embody a maxim to which he remained faithful when he faced the history of the Roman Empire. For if he was later vain both of his person and of his reputation, it was never to the prejudice of the volumes which he constructed with such architectural art.

Having finished the *Essay*, Gibbon asked for an opinion of it from Dr. Maty. "Can you believe" he wrote to Maty "that a man born to assist at the tumultuous meetings of parliament, and to destroy the foxes in his county, will be pardoned for discussing what was thought, two thousand years ago, about the divinities of Greece, and the early ages of Rome?"—a passage which shows another side to the cultured English aristocracy of the eighteenth century, for it might have been written by one of the Sitwells in condemnation of the Edwardian upper class. It echoes Gibbon's boredom with Hampshire society, but it is true that at this time he had hardly penetrated the more cultivated circles of the capital, in which he was to be more at home.

Maty approved the *Essai sur l'étude de la littérature*, adding some words of his own commendation, and it was published under this title in 1761. Copies were sent abroad, where not unnaturally it received more notice than in London. Looking back on it in later life, Gibbon was not dissatisfied, finding in it "some dawnings of a philosophic spirit", and as with him "philosophy" is often used in opposition to religion, this affords another indication that his opinions were not yet fixed.

Yet he was also surprised, as other artists and writers have been, in trying to review their youthful works with a superior spirit, to find how far he had already advanced:

> Upon the whole, I may apply to the first labour of my pen the speech of a far superior artist, when he surveyed the first productions of his pencil. After viewing some portraits which he had painted in his youth, my friend Sir Joshua Reynolds acknowledged to me that he was rather humbled than flattered by the comparison with his present works: and that after so much time and study, he had conceived his improvement to be much greater than he found it to have been. (*Autobiography*, p. 101.)

This may seem further evidence that the experiences which he had already suffered at Lausanne had done much to form the essential Gibbon, and that the spirit in which he wrote his history owed more to them than to the reading he later devoted to it. His opinions were not yet finally fixed, but they had already developed.

Gibbon received his first printed copy of the *Essay* when taking the field with the Hampshire militia, which was to engage the rest of his time before the Grand Tour. A national militia had long been the wish of the Tories and the country squires, "who insensibly transferred their loyalty to the house of Hanover", as had the Gibbons themselves. The colonel of the South Hampshire Grenadiers was Sir Thomas Worsley, Gibbon's father was major of the battalion, and Gibbon was in charge of a company. But although he was only a captain, his two superior officers were so often absent or idle that most of the responsibility devolved upon him, and he accepted this with the same readiness, and discharged it with the same thoroughness as he responded to every call of fate.

The battalion marched over southern England and was quartered in a number of towns for which Gibbon found an appropriate epithet, from "pleasant and hospitable Blandford" in Dorset, to the "populous and disorderly town of Devizes", and to Dover where it "exercised in sight of the Gallic shores". He even found an appropriate epithet for the South Hampshire Grenadiers themselves, as their motto, *Falces Conflantur in Enses*, an apt one for ploughboys who had taken the sword, is ascribed to him. Gibbon swelled into pride for his regiment and noted that when it was encamped on Winchester Down, "in the general reviews the South Hampshire were rather a credit than a disgrace to the line".

At one time he was so stirred as to consider becoming a regular soldier: "But this military fever was cooled by the enjoyment of our mimic Bellona, who soon unveiled to my eyes her naked deformity." He was bored by the company of his fox-hunting fellow-officers, and he grudged the time wasted from his reading. Soldiering lost its charms, but he gained an insight into the character of soldiers, as he showed in Chapter VII of *The Decline and Fall*, where he noted that "the temper of soldiers, habituated at once to violence and to slavery, renders them very unfit guardians of a legal, or even a civil, constitution". (i, p. 182.)

In his memoirs he recognized this debt to his battalion:

> The discipline and evolution of a modern battalion gave me a clearer notion of the phalanx and the legion; and the captain of the Hampshire grenadiers (the reader may smile) has not been useless to the historian of the Roman Empire.
>
> (*Autobiography*, p. 106.)

One example of this was his observation of the difference between the establishment of a regiment and the number of men actually under arms. In the grand review on Winchester Down, the assembled regiments had little more than half their establishment. Gibbon reflected that the discrepancy must be even greater in foreign service, and it is perhaps from such instances as this that he learnt his caution in accepting figures, not only of troops in the field of history, but also of Christian martyrs.

Nor were his literary studies neglected. The militia was embodied in 1760, and it is to the following year that his *Journal* assigns his *Critical Researches Concerning the Title of Charles VIII to the Crown of Naples*. His reading was wide, and it was with relief that he turned to that from carousing in the mess. One "very debauched day" was enlivened by the presence of Colonel John Wilkes of the Buckinghamshire militia: "I scarcely ever met with a better companion; he has inexhaustible spirits, infinite wit and humour, and a great deal of knowledge; but a thorough profligate in principle as in practice, his life stained with every vice, and his conversation full of blasphemy and indecency." (*Journal*, 23 Sept. 1762.) This may be a fair enough estimate of Wilkes, but it is also a reflection of Gibbon's own character, which was more respectable, not only in practice but also in principle, than has always been allowed by his critics.

Towards the end of 1762 the militia was disbanded, leaving Gibbon free to resume his intellectual and social pursuits. His *Journal* (26 November 1762) records:

I went with Mallet to breakfast with Garrick: and thence to Drury Lane house, where I assisted at a very private rehearsal, in the Green Room, of a new tragedy of Mallet's, called *Elvira*.

A few weeks later on 19 January 1763, Gibbon went to the
first night:

> My father and I went to the Rose, in the passage of the
> play-house, where we found Mallet, with about thirty friends.
> We dined together, and went thence into the pit, where we
> took our places in a body, ready to silence all opposition.
> However, we had no occasion to exert ourselves. Not-
> withstanding the malice of party, Mallet's nation, con-
> nexions, and, indeed, imprudence, we heard nothing but
> applause. I think it was deserved.

Gibbon admitted the justice of criticism against confusion
in the climax of the play, but said that he was himself much
more struck by "the dreadful situation of a father who condemns
his son to death". He devoted half a page to discussing this,
arguing that only high motives of public policy could justify
such paternal severity—a subject on which experience had
given him some reason to meditate.

It is possible that, by introducing him to David Mallet, his
father had affected his life almost as decisively as in the earlier
intervention, when he had also carried him off to the Mallets'
house in Putney. It is less easy to estimate the real worth of
Mallet, whose career has not received the study which it
perhaps deserves. Some regarded him as excessively vain, but
vanity is often attributed, not always justly, to men who press
their opinions with an excess of confidence. He was small in
stature, and assertive by nature. He had worked with James
Thomson on a masque, *Alfred*, and after Thomson's death
used to claim that the work was preponderantly his own, which
for a time gained him the reputation of having written "Rule
Britannia". His poetry had sufficient merit to be edited anew
in the middle of the nineteenth century, and one of his poems,

"The Birks of Endermay", appears in a standard anthology of British verse. Its concluding lines are:

> Our taste of pleasure then is o'er,
> The feathered songsters love no more;
> And when they droop and we decay,
> Adieu the shades of Endermay!

But whatever Mallet's real merit, his opinions, for which, as Sheffield said, a stronger term than "deistical" might have been employed, influenced the younger mind of Gibbon. Already, while serving with the militia, Gibbon had read Cicero's *On the Nature of the Gods*, which has so often been a manual for sceptics, with its reminder that all the problems of human destiny had been discussed with as little agreement by the ancients as by the moderns. He could regard himself as an apostle of the Enlightenment, and he had considered writing a history of the liberty of the Swiss—both Bayle and Le Clerc had resided in Geneva before settling in Holland. The knowledge he had acquired had prepared him for the greater French Enlightenment which he was to encounter in Paris, but it also made him more sophisticated in his approach to it, for to him it was no novelty. Yet the opinions he already had were formed on French models, those of the French exiles in Holland, of whom his Dr. Maty was a less famous representative, developed with some inspiration from the Scots, such as Hume and Mallet himself.

Relieved of the militia, Gibbon was at last free to embark on the Grand Tour, to which he had so long been straining. Even in this Mallet was of service, providing him with letters for friends in Paris. Lady Hervey, to whom Mallet had presented him, and the Duke of Nivernois, introduced by Maty, added more.

Yet his time in the militia had not been wasted, for it had made him at home in his own country and in his own language. When he went abroad again, it was with his stock of learning increased and his French unimpaired, but it was also with the confidence of a man who knew where he stood. In 1763, at the age of twenty-six, he was ready for his life's work.

He went first to Paris, which was then the capital of Europe. It is difficult to exaggerate the influence of France and the French language both on the intellectual climate of the eighteenth century and on the mind of Gibbon. Rivarol asserted with justice that the language was so clear and reasonable that it was no longer French, but the speech of the human race, and it had so penetrated the civilized mind that De Maistre could claim that a work of propaganda written in French was a weapon discharged with the strength of a hundred thousand men, as its effect was felt far beyond the national frontiers.

It was in fact in propaganda that the French writers of the later eighteenth century excelled, following the classical verse and art of Louis XIV's reign, whose prestige they inherited; a propaganda directed against established institutions, both political and religious, which had either fossilized or grown corrupt. So France, though outwardly still a monarchy and a Catholic country, exercised the same influence over intellectuals as Soviet Russia had over a generation now passing. This liberalizing movement of propaganda, the Enlightenment, held out the same prospect of a new world and a heaven on earth, once the dead forms of the past had been destroyed, and it therefore demanded the same rewriting of history, which led to an attack not only on existing corruptions, but on the origins of the institutions themselves.

This distinction between the corrupt form and the original thing, between kings and monarchy, between bishops and religion, between absentee landlords and property, was not always clear either to the attackers or to the attacked, but it is a necessary distinction, for without it the Enlightenment appears a more united movement than it really was; before a revolution, there is usually a measure of agreement among reformers, who differ and often fight to the death only when the revolution is over and they are free to build their new world. So the writers of the Encyclopaedia, who aimed to produce a new body of enlightened knowledge, and the great names of the movement, a Diderot, a D'Alembert, a Voltaire, differed among themselves. When the French Revolution came, people said that it was "the fault of Voltaire, the fault of Rousseau", confusing Voltaire's eighteenth-century sophistication and cynicism with Rousseau's cult of nature, which was largely a reaction against those qualities.

Gibbon was evidently influenced by French criticism, but he had already been initiated into the Enlightenment some years before he made his visit to Paris in 1763. French influences would be exaggerated if his opinion of Rousseau and Voltaire were overlooked. Apart from his personal difference with Rousseau over Suzanne Curchod, noted above, he had little feeling for nature, which was one point on which he could agree with the "bigoted" Dr. Johnson, of whom Boswell wrote in his *Tour of the Hebrides*: "We had a pleasant conviction of the commodiousness of civilisation, and heartily laughed at the ravings of those absurd visionaries who have attempted to persuade us of the superior advantages of a state of nature." Gibbon had as small an opinion of the ravings of Rousseau, whom he "pitied" as much as he admired.

As for Voltaire, already in Lausanne Gibbon had seen "the most extraordinary man of the age . . . whom I then rated above his real magnitude". He had even seen Voltaire acting in his own plays at Monrepos, in a suburb of Lausanne, and had been received by him personally. But while he regarded Voltaire's works as "often excellent, and always entertaining", he could not pardon his inaccuracy. In view of the influence on Gibbon with which Voltaire has been credited, it is perhaps useful to bring together some of Gibbon's references to him in *The Decline and Fall*:

In Chapter I: "M. de Voltaire, unsupported by either fact or probability, has generously bestowed the Canary Islands on the Roman Empire." (i, p. 28.)

In Chapter XLVII: ". . . La Croze, Voltaire, etc., who become the dupes of their own cunning, while they are afraid of a Jesuitical fraud." (v, p. 160*n*.)

In Chapter LII: " . . . the mistakes of Voltaire proceeded from the want of knowledge or reflection." (vi, p. 23.)

In Chapter LIII: "Voltaire might wonder at this alliance; but he should not have owned his ignorance of the country, religion, etc, of Jeroslaus . . ." (vi, p. 93.)

In Chapter LXVII: "In his way, Voltaire was a bigot, an intolerant bigot." (vii, p. 146*n*.)

This last phrase is hardly less strong than Gibbon's condemnation of Dr. Johnson. In his *Journal*, before the visit to Paris, there is a further note that Voltaire, when writing of a distant period, "produces a most agreeable, superficial, inaccurate performance". The *Journal* contains a more friendly reference to Erasmus, and just as Erasmus was a moderate as far as the reform of the Church was concerned, so Gibbon held back from the political reforms of the Enlightenment, whose more extreme elements were too close to the "enthusiasm" for which he had such repugnance.

Even in his irony, Gibbon was more influenced by Pascal: "From the *Provincial Letters* of Pascal, which almost every year I have perused with new pleasure, I learned to manage the weapon of grave and temperate irony, even on subjects of ecclesiastical solemnity." (*Autobiography*, p. 75.) His sources were French, but they preceded Voltaire, and perhaps one of the first inspirations of *The Decline and Fall* was Montesquieu's *Considérations sur les causes de la grandeur des Romains et leur décadence*, which was published in 1734.

It was French scholarship, more than French criticism, which impressed Gibbon, and one of his first visits in Paris was to the Abbey of St.-Germain-des-Prés, whose Benedictine folios he contrasted so favourably with the emptiness and idleness of Magdalen and Oxford. He was in fact singularly free from national prejudice, and if he had the prejudices of his age, he was far from the "bigotry" of which he accused Voltaire.

Most of Gibbon's critics have insisted on French influences in him, but perhaps the one who saw this most clearly was Cotter Morison, whose own life in the nineteenth century formed a parallel to his. Morison's father had made a fortune and then settled in Paris, so that the son had the same background of wealth as Gibbon's grandfather had made for him. Morison himself had, like Gibbon, been attracted to Catholicism but, again like Gibbon, had rejected it in favour of the philosophy of his age, in his case positivism. His friend John Morley wrote of his being "passionately concerned in Catholicism, not as a body of faith and rite, but as a stupendous system of government with profound significance in the annals of mankind. He longed, as in truth any of us well might, for the historian to arise who, as he used to say, would depict with sweeping brush the Decline and Fall of Theological, as Gibbon of Imperial, Rome."

The fascination of this to an age with still other prejudices is its illustration that the history of Rome presents different facets according to the philosophy of the observer. Gibbon, with his respect for government, saw Rome in that context, while Morison, with his positivism, was drawn to its religious organization. But both men saw it as central to the European scene, and although they did not share its religion, they viewed this from the standpoint, not of English, but of French, sceptics.

This digression into Morison's outlook is justified if it clarifies a fine shade in Gibbon's scepticism; he had none of that respect for Christianity which often remains with Englishmen who have rejected religion, nor was rationalism a religion with him as it was with some Victorians. He had more of the detachment of the French sceptic, who concedes religion as useful to women and children, and perhaps to peasants, but unworthy of the superior and intellectual man.

It is this, no less than the fact, on which Morison insisted, that his culture was "chiefly French", which makes Gibbon the most un-English of great English writers, a judgment in which Morison has been joined by Mr. Christopher Dawson.

Yet when Gibbon was in Paris in 1763, he had already been turned into an Englishman by the militia, and it was as an English man of fashion that he wished to be regarded. Fortunately his Anglo-French mind was in the intellectual fashion, since Locke had influenced French political writers, "and every Englishman" as Gibbon wrote "was supposed to be a patriot and a philosopher". His name was known to Paris through his *Essay*, but though flattered he was a little piqued to be received as a man of letters rather than a man of fashion. In his *Journal* for this year he noted, on a satire of Juvenal, "the poverty and contempt attending the men of letters of his times. The subject is always a disagreeable one . . ." He dressed carefully and made good use of his introductions, soon pleased to find that there were more doors open to him in Paris than in London: "I was a recognised man of letters, and it is only in Paris that this quality forms a distinct status." Yet he remained English enough to wish the gentleman to take precedence.

He also affected that English attitude to the French which

he expressed so admirably in Chapter XXXVIII of *The Decline and Fall*: "Perhaps the Franks already displayed the social disposition, and lively graces, which in every age, have disguised their vices, and sometimes concealed their intrinsic merit." (iv, p. 129.)

It was while he was in Paris that the equestrian statue of Louis XV was set up in the square to bear his name, now the Place de la Concorde. The mob, with that "lively grace" that Gibbon noted as typical of the Franks, declared that it would never pass the house of Madame de Pompadour.

From Paris he moved to Lausanne, which had already been so decisive a stage in his life—now a stage in his path to Rome.

VII

THE PATH TO ROME

After a sleepless night, I trod, with a lofty step, the ruins of the Forum; each memorable spot where Romulus *stood*, or Tully spoke, or Caesar fell, was at once present to my eye; and several days of intoxication were lost or enjoyed before I could descend to a cool and minute investigation.

(*Autobiography*, p. 159.)

IN Lausanne, where he remained for nearly a year, Gibbon had more leisure to examine both his character and his opinions than had been possible in the social round of Paris. Already in the previous year he had used his twenty-sixth birthday to consider such questions:

This gave me occasion to look a little into myself, and consider impartially my good and bad qualities. It appeared to me, upon this inquiry, that my character was virtuous, incapable of a base action, and formed for generous ones; but that it was proud, violent, and disagreeable in society. These qualities I must endeavour to cultivate, extirpate, or restrain, according to their different tendency. Wit I have none. My imagination is rather strong than pleasing. My memory both capacious and retentive. The shining qualities of my understanding are extensiveness and penetration; but I want both quickness and exactness. As to my situation in life, though I may sometimes repine at it, it perhaps is the best adapted to my character. I can command all the

96

conveniences of life, and I can command too that independence (that first earthly blessing), which is hardly to be met with in a higher or lower fortune.

(*Journal*, 8 May 1762.)

His skill in introspection was less striking than some passages in his memoirs might suggest. He was rarely hypocritical—except in his famous letter to Priestley—and he well balanced his merits against his defects, but his uncertainty on motives made him an ill judge of behaviour. He was rather "base" than "generous" in his treatment of Suzanne. His modesty was equally inexact, for his contemporaries concur on his great social gifts, and a critic who said that Gibbon had no wit would be as much discounted as one who said that Shakespeare had no poetry.

But when he wrote the passage quoted above, he was more uncertain than in his maturity, and his *Journal* betrays a similar uncertainty in the progress of his opinions, for there are subtle changes recorded in the year 1763. In December he wrote respectfully of Communion in Lausanne, "a very edifying spectacle". Two months before this occurred another passage, of interest not only in that context but also in relation to *The Decline and Fall*, the plan of which he had not yet conceived:

. . . the inhabitants of Germany, the Goths, Vandals, and Franks, had divested themselves of much of their barbarism before they invaded the dominions of the Roman Empire. For more than a century preceding that event, numerous bodies of their countrymen had served in the Roman armies. They learned the Latin language; they adopted civilised manners; and if they were not Christians, they at least revered Christianity. (*Journal*, 6 Oct. 1763.)

In the following month he noted a book on four hundred likenesses of St. Francis and Christ, to comment in a tone more like the later Gibbon's, that "the absurdity of this book gives it a kind of value". It is another French trait in him that he was rather attracted than shocked by what he regarded as absurd in religious writings, for he had more the detached amusement of an observer than the zeal of a reformer.

At the end of the year he wrote: "I hope to be able to give a description of ancient Italy", another hint of the work ahead.

It is in the following year, 1764, that his *Journal* betrays more evident signs of the authentic Gibbon. In reading the Abbé Fleury's *Method and Choice of our Studies*, he observed: "The author was a Roman Catholic and a priest; but this fault is perceived by those only who are neither the one nor the other." Then he noted of the *New Aretin* that it "would be thrown by with disgust, did it not attack religion with the most shocking indecency". These notes occur in February and March 1764. In June there are two which suggest a balance between earlier and later opinions. The first might have been written by a Christian, one more Catholic than Protestant in outlook: "All religions depend in some degree on local circumstances. The least superstitious Christian would feel more devotion on Mount Calvary than in London." The second, referring to the development of Christianity, might well have found a place in *The Decline and Fall*: "Bishops, priests, and women, who mingled caresses with controversy, were sedulous to convert the princes and great men, whose example was easily followed by that of the careless multitude." (*Journal*, 16 June 1764.)

This was written a month after he had left Lausanne, where he stayed nearly eleven months, but these notes give some indication that his opinions were again changing there, or finally evaporating into the ethereal deism which remained his philosophy. Some have argued that he passed beyond that and was nearer to Hume in his scepticism, but his famous Chapters XV and XVI on Christianity are written from the standpoint of a deist, and his references to Islam suggest a deist sympathy, as in Chapter LI, when he wrote that "the religion of Mahomet might seem less inconsistent with reason than the creed of mystery and superstition, which in the seventh century disgraced the simplicity of the Gospel". (v, p. 517.) There was a grain of truth in Johnson's laughing remark, " 'Tis said he has been a Mohammedan", for the deists were closer to the Mohammedans than to the Christians. Most of the French intellectuals were also deists, and it is possible that what Gibbon did share with Voltaire was his religious philosophy.

This second stay of Gibbon's in Lausanne was also important in that he made the acquaintance of Holroyd, later Lord Sheffield, who remained for life his closest and most helpful friend, finally the executor of his will and the editor of his memoirs. Gibbon learnt to appreciate Holroyd's character and good sense in steps which they took together to avert a foolish duel between two of their acquaintances. He welcomed Holroyd's company in Lausanne the more as his friend Deyverdun was absent in Germany.

From Lausanne he moved south in the summer of 1764: "Rome is the great object of our pilgrimage." In crossing the Alps he was reminded of Hannibal's elephants descending upon Italy:

I climbed Mount Cenis, and descended into the plain of Piedmont, not on the back of an elephant, but on a light osier seat, in the hands of the dexterous and intrepid chairmen of the Alps.   (*Autobiography*, p. 143.)

At Genoa he met and was entertained by the Celesias. Mallet's daughter Dorothy, a child of his first wife, had escaped as soon as possible from the "tyranny" of her stepmother, who was perhaps too conscious of her wealth and her father's stewardship to the Earl of Carlisle, by marrying Celesia, the Genoese envoy in London, and had returned with him to Genoa. Dorothy Celesia had inherited her father's literary gifts, and later herself had a play shown in London, owing to the good offices of Garrick. Both she and her husband made Gibbon very welcome and instructed him in the affairs of Genoa and Corsica, then under the rule of Boswell's hero Paoli, whom they compared to Cromwell, alike in puritanism and in ambition.

From Genoa he moved to Florence, where his outlook on art was enlarged, as there he "acknowledged at the feet of the Venus of Medicis, that the chisel may dispute the pre-eminence with the pencil, a truth in the fine arts which cannot on this side of the Alps be felt or understood". (*Autobiography*, p. 150.) But what interested him most at Florence were the busts of the Roman emperors, many of whom he listed in his *Journal*, which he was keeping in French, the language of Europe in that century, natural to him after his months in Lausanne. It was with a lively pleasure that he contemplated these likenesses of the world's masters, only regretting that each bust did not have beside it a drawer of medals to facilitate comparisons.

In Julius Caesar he was struck by the shrunken features, the hollow cheeks, the marks of age. It was difficult to believe that he was a man who had died at the early age of fifty-six. Yet his celebrated baldness was not shown in the bust, although the hair was sparse.

An excellent bust of Caligula impressed by its exact re-semblances to medals of the tyrant. The features were very mature, for a man who died at thirty.

In Nero's bust he found much expression, but of an uncertain sort, perhaps because he confessed that Nero had never
disgusted him as much as Tiberius, Caligula, or Domitian.
He had many vices, but he was not lacking in virtues. Gibbon
found small trace of deliberate wickedness in his life. He was
cruel, but more through fear than by choice.

Vitellius, the glutton, had appropriately fleshy features.
Gibbon was surprised that many likenesses of this emperor
had survived, and put it down to Vespasian's contempt for him.
Vespasian's head was one of singular fineness, although rather
ugly than handsome. It was an entirely human face, gay, calm
and majestic in expression. Gibbon was convinced that it was
an exact likeness.

Trajan's bust was remarkable for its mocking smile.

Hadrian's was also striking—the first of the emperors to
allow his beard to grow, although he had it trimmed, not letting
it develop into the full-flowing beard in which the philosophers
of the age took such pride.

There were three busts of Marcus Aurelius, of which Gibbon
preferred the one which showed him as a young man and noted
that all that family's busts were more impressive in the details
of the features than in their general expression.

The total number of busts, not confined to emperors,
which Gibbon examined over the course of days was ninety-
two.

He also went to the church of Santa Croce, whose architecture did not impress him. But he showed respect for the tombs
of Michelangelo and Galileo, bowing before their power and
originality in art and philosophy. He considered that they
were a greater glory to their country than any conquerors or
politicians. The Tartars had their Jenghis Khan and the Goths
their Alaric, but it was with pleasure that Gibbon turned his
eyes from the bloody plains of Scythia to rest on the glories of

Athens and Florence—a phrase suited to the style of *The Decline and Fall*.

The traveller was becoming absorbed in the historian. "Without engaging in a metaphysical or rather verbal dispute, I *know*, by experience, that from my early youth I aspired to the character of an historian." (*Autobiography*, p. 117.)

On the way to Rome he encountered at Pisa his Acton relations, and pitied the poor old man, who was avoided by the English owing to his change of religion, yet had not learnt the Italian tongue of his fellow-Papists, as unhappy as Macaulay's Jacobite who "pined by Arno for his lovelier Tees".

Then, in October, Gibbon was at last in Rome, from where he wrote to his father, of the Romans: "Whatever ideas books may have given us of the greatness of that people, their accounts of the most flourishing state of Rome fall infinitely short of the picture of its ruins."

Perhaps they only fell short of the more magnificent picture which Gibbon was to draw in his own book, for it was among those ruins that the first vision of *The Decline and Fall* "started to my mind", that first vision which to a writer is always more impressive than the finished work, however skilfully accomplished.

Gibbon's feelings when confronted with the monuments of Rome have been sufficiently considered and nowhere better described than in the pages of his *Autobiography* and in the final chapter of *The Decline and Fall*. What is most remarkable is the persistence and single-mindedness with which he overcame the obstacles of time and space in order to become intimate with the history and the topography of Rome. It might indeed be argued that the chief defects in his character were due to the ruthlessness with which he pursued these objects, and to criticize him adequately would be to analyse the character of his favourite emperors, who so influenced him in his Olympian calm, in his deep respect for administrative virtues, and in his indifference to qualities outside the closed Roman world of civilization—his refusal to believe in the other world. His own bust would not have been out of place in that corridor in Florence, perhaps close to the head of Vespasian, which was rather ugly than handsome—Vespasian, whose last words were so Gibbonian in their scepticism and irony: "Alas, I suppose I am turning into a god."

His persistence in at last reaching Rome was the more surprising in view of the difficulties of travelling at that time, which demanded so much endurance and exertion, to which Gibbon was at all times singularly averse. His physical constitution became more and more phlegmatic; he had already contracted the hydrocele (while serving with the militia) which years later was to prove fatal, and this increased his constitutional dislike of exercise in any form. He was by nature a scholar in a library. Yet he reached Rome. To this contrast between his nature and that of a traveller he made an amusing reference in his *Autobiography* (p. 160):

The use of foreign travel has been often debated as a general question; but the conclusion must be finally applied to the character and circumstances of each individual. With the education of boys, *where* or *how* they may pass over some juvenile years with the least mischief to themselves or others, I have no concern. But after supposing the previous and indispensable requisites of age, judgement, a competent knowledge of men and books, and a freedom from domestic prejudices, I will briefly describe the qualifications which I deem most essential to a traveller. He should be endowed with an active, indefatigable vigour of mind and body, which can seize every mode of conveyance, and support, with a careless smile, every hardship of the road, the weather, or the inn. The benefits of foreign travel will correspond with the degrees of these qualifications; but, in this sketch, those to whom I am known will not accuse me of framing my own panegyric.

Yet in spite of his physical lethargy, he not only devoted eighteen weeks to the tour of Rome, but even went to Naples:

> Six weeks were borrowed for my tour of Naples, the most populous of cities, relative to its size, whose various inhabitants seem to dwell on the confines of paradise and hell-fire. . . . On my return, I fondly embraced, for the last time, the miracles of Rome. . . .
>
> (*Autobiography*, p. 159.)

From Rome he returned by Lyons to Paris, and so to Dover, the end of a tour which had not only fixed the cast of his mind, but furnished him with his life's work. His scepticism had been increased by his travels, for just as in his childhood and youth he had never remained long in one place, nor taken root, except during his exile at Lausanne, so also his mind had never had time to settle in any system of belief. Faith may grow from childhood, or it may be achieved in youth or later by a sudden revolution, but scepticism is more often a slow process of change, comparable to the decline of Rome. Often enough it is accompanied by the strengthening of a new belief in a lower order of reality, social, personal or scientific. The stronger element of Gibbon's new belief was perhaps less deism than respect for the civilization and order of which Rome was the supreme representative. As he wrote in Chapter LV of *The Decline and Fall* on the conversion of the Slavs, he had "imbibed the free and generous spirit of the European republic". (vi, p. 173.) It was a quality which enlarged his outlook and informed his work, giving him a breadth unique among English historians. "Our antiquarians" he could loftily but not unjustly observe in Chapter XXXI "have been betrayed into many gross errors by their imperfect knowledge of the history of the continent." (iii, p. 372.)

He had already travelled and studied to repair that deficiency, and thenceforward he settled down to extend his own and his countrymen's knowledge of European history through the Roman Empire, on which the history of Europe was based.

VIII

STUDY AND SOCIETY

I had now attained the first of earthly blessings, independence: I was the absolute master of my hours and actions: nor was I deceived in the hope that the establishment of my library in town would allow me to divide the day between study and society. Each year the circle of my acquaintance, the number of my dead and living companions, was enlarged.

(Autobiography, p. 176.)

THE optimism of the passage cited above, which refers to the year 1772, when Gibbon at last had his own home in London, was far from the state of mind in which he returned to his father's house in the summer of 1765, at the age of twenty-eight. He relates that the five and a half years between his return from the tour and his father's death in 1770 were "the portion of my life which I passed with the least enjoyment, and which I remember with the least satisfaction" (p. 161). But this sombre reference was perhaps less occasioned by any unhappiness than by his impatience to settle down to the historical writing on which he had set his heart.

He was further burdened with the yearly exercises of the militia, for his father had dropped out, raising him to the rank of major, and when Worsley died he became the battalion's commanding officer. Nor was "Colonel Gibbon" ever at home in the country; but the summer months there were relieved by visits from his friend Deyverdun, and the winter was spent in London, where he was consoled by new acquaintances made on his travels or in the militia, and by weekly gatherings of the Roman Club, the name given to a circle of those who had made the Grand Tour, among them his friend Holroyd and the future Lord Bute. But he missed Mallet, who had died in the year of his return from the tour.

It was a life which might have been far more agreeable than the sickness and trials of his earlier years, but he was vexed by the frustration of his ambition. "While so many of my acquaintance were married or in parliament, or advancing with a rapid step in the various roads of honour and fortune, I stood alone, immovable and insignificant . . ." The confidence that he had acquired in the awareness of his gifts only made it more galling to him that he had as yet done nothing with them. He was in the wilderness, while others had found either their vocation or their path to fame:

> I lamented that at the proper age I had not embraced the lucrative pursuits of the law or of trade, the chances of civil office or India adventure, or even the fat slumbers of the church; and my repentance became more lively as the loss of time was more irretrievable.
>
> (*Autobiography*, p. 163.)

Even in those days when private enterprise had so much larger a scope, he could note a fact which is more acutely evident to young men today: "Experience showed me the use of grafting my private consequence on the importance of a great professional body . . ."

The real cause of this malaise was that, while he cherished the plan of *The Decline and Fall*, he had not yet acquired either the leisure or the determination to work on it. The limitations of his life, and the awe with which he regarded that majestic subject, oppressed him with fear and checked the optimistic resolution necessary to so great a task. Yet he both needed to write and was aware of his ability to carry out some historical work. After consultations with Deyverdun, he decided on a history of the Swiss republics, of which the first part was written and read to a literary society in London. Deyverdun conveyed it to Hume, who wrote to Gibbon with approval, saying that it was written "with spirit and judgement". But criticism from others discouraged him and he abandoned the work. Next he joined with Deyverdun in compiling some historical memoirs, but these activities also lapsed when he secured for Deyverdun the post of tutor to his former colonel's son. In 1770 he published *Critical Observations on the Sixth Book of the Aeneid*, an attack on Bishop Warburton, who had sought to prove that Virgil was here revealing secrets of the Eleusinian mysteries, which Gibbon regarded as "equally injurious to the poet and the man".

But these scattered activities were of far less account than the reading which was now systematically taking him into the Roman Empire, above all the *Histoire des empereurs* of Tillemont, whose works were to be so useful a companion to him through the first three volumes of *The Decline and Fall*.

These studies were interrupted in the summer of 1770 by the condition of his father:

My quiet was gradually disturbed by our domestic anxiety, and I should be ashamed of my unfeeling philosophy had I found much time to waste for study in the last fatal summer of my father's decay and dissolution.

(*Autobiography*, p. 173.)

This father's character emerges clearly enough from the pages of Gibbon's memoirs. One jocular reference to "the

Major" relieves the filial respect that Gibbon had always displayed, even to the loss of his faith and of his love. But that one reference to "the Major" is enough, revealing the trace of amiable absurdity in his character. He had maintained his authority, but he had been unable to manage his property, most of which was mortgaged, "and each year multiplied the number, and exhausted the patience of his creditors". At his death, Gibbon made the last of his submissions: "I submitted to the order of nature; and my grief was soothed by the conscious satisfaction that I had discharged all the duties of filial piety." (*Autobiography*, p. 175.)

His next task was to disentangle the network of mortgages and achieve the independent life in London which was his first desire. This took two years, though the final clearing of the estates lasted for most of his life, and much of the work devolved upon Holroyd, when Gibbon was out of the country. It was not until 1772, at the mature age of thirty-five, that Gibbon settled in London and at once began work on the first volume of *The Decline and Fall*, whose final volume was to be achieved fifteen years later in the summer-house at Lausanne.

At last he had his independence, "the first of earthly blessings", which was to be the masterly quality of his finished work. He had also escaped from the inertia of country life, which had so little appeal for him. A few months before reaching his haven in London he had written to Holroyd: "You will ever remain a bigot to those Rustic Deities; I propose to abjure them soon, and to reconcile myself to the Catholic Church of London." The phrase was lightly written, but it was a true reflection of the cosmopolitan spirit in him: whenever he was remote from the confines of a city, he had the nostalgia of a Roman banished to a distant province in the ultimate region of Britain or the Black Sea, and even when he left England Lausanne had for him the metropolitan charm of a Rome.

In the following year, 1773, he could write from London, "I lead the true life of a Philosopher which consists in doing what I really like without any regard to the world or to fashion." (7 August 1773.)

Yet he was far from neglecting fashion, either in his appearance or in his pursuits. He had become so much the English gentleman that he had no longer the same need to insist on the fact as in Paris. He even found that London, in that enlightened age, had hardly less respect for polite letters than Paris, so that he was able to refine his ideas of gentility and admire the family of Confucius as the most respectable on this planet, though at heart he was with the aristocracy—a prejudice later strengthened in him by the outbreak of the French Revolution.

These ten years, from 1773 to 1783, when he left England for Lausanne, the years between his middle thirties and his middle forties which so often decide a man's position in the world, were for Gibbon the period of achievement, literary, social and public. They were marked above all by the publication in 1776 of the first volume of *The Decline and Fall*, which had an immediate and a striking success, shedding lustre on the man of fashion and the Member of Parliament (to which he had been elected two years before). They were the years in which he became a public figure, with his snuff-box, his urbanity, his polished conversation, "the characteristics of which" Lord Sheffield wrote "were vivacity, elegance, and precision, with knowledge astonishingly extensive and correct. He never ceased to be instructive and entertaining; and in general there was a vein of pleasantry in his conversation which prevented its becoming languid . . ." He was the friendly historian known to his readers, the attractive writer of his memoirs, of which Sheffield's sister wrote: "They make me feel affectionate to Mr. Gibbon."

These were the public years, in which portraits of him were painted. That by Henry Walton, possibly made in 1774, shows a large round face, double chin, big, alert eyes with heavy brows. These eyes are confident, with a sparkle of humourous malice; the nose a blob, earning for him the nick-name of "The Potato". But the Reynolds portrait of 1779 shows a nose more finely tipped, that of a terrier on the scent, ready to quiver with quick interest. Most observers noted his vivacity, a quality which is always the one which makes a likeness an injustice to its subject, so inseparable is it from the living person.

The Walton portrait might be that of an alderman, the Reynolds that of a cabinet minister, one of dignity and perhaps of genius. But the chief qualities of that genius, its quickness and liveliness, were not to be fixed in paint.

Of these years, Gibbon wrote:

> The militia, my travels, the House of Commons, the fame of an author contributed to multiply my connections: I was chosen a member of the fashionable clubs; and, before I left England in 1783, there were few persons of any eminence in the literary or political world to whom I was a stranger.
> (*Autobiography*, p. 176.)

Yet despite the public and fashionable life, which extended his confidence and his serenity, he remained, as Sir A. W. Ward remarks, "a perfect type of the literary mind proper". He himself brought out the fact in a reference to his clubs: "From the mixed, though polite company of Boodle's, White's and Brook's, I must honourably distinguish a weekly society, which was instituted in the year 1764, and which still continues to flourish, under the title of the Literary Club." This was the Club famous to readers of Boswell's *Johnson*, which also included Burke, Fox, Sheridan, Reynolds, Garrick, Goldsmith and Adam Smith—"a large and luminous constellation of British stars."

Among the lesser stars was George Colman, whose son, ignored by Johnson, left a description of the two greater literary figures which few writers on Gibbon have been able to let pass, so vivid is its resurrection of his vivacity:

The learned Gibbon was a curious counterbalance to the learned (may I not say the less learned) Johnson. Their manners and tastes, both in writing and conversation, were as different as their habiliments. On the day I first sat down with Johnson in his rusty-brown suit and his black worsted stockings, Gibbon was placed opposite to me in a suit of flowered velvet, with a bag and sword. Each had his measured phraseology, and Johnson's famous parallel between Dryden and Pope might be loosely parodied in reference to himself and Gibbon. Johnson's style was grand, and Gibbon's elegant: the stateliness of the former was sometimes pedantic, and the latter was occasionally finical. Johnson marched to kettledrums and trumpets, Gibbon moved to flutes and hautboys. Johnson hewd passages through the Alps, while Gibbon levelled walks through parks and gardens. Mauled as I had been by Johnson, Gibbon poured balm upon my bruises by condescending once or twice in the course of the evening to talk with me. The great historian was light and playful, suiting his matter to the capacity of the boy: but it was done *more suo*—still his mannerism prevailed, still he tapped his snuff-box, still he smirked and smiled, and rounded his periods with the same air of good-breeding, as if he were conversing with men. His mouth, mellifluous as Plato's, was a round hole nearly in the centre of his visage.

This "round hole" has caused some speculation. The image was perhaps occasioned by the shock of fine phrases emerging from a mouth set between a double chin and a featureless nose—as today when a man speaks into a microphone, this round object diverts the attention of those seated in front of him from the rest of his face. For it was certainly the charm of his conversation which drew people to Gibbon, and it was the contrast between the liveliness of his words and the commonplace features which caused friendly amusement in some and malice in others. In Colman, meeting it for the first time, it simply caused surprise, which he well expressed in his image of the "round hole".

Among his other clubs Gibbon had acquired membership of one which to some, though not all, of its members, was something more than a club—the House of Commons. He obtained his seat at Liskeard in Cornwall through the friendship of his cousin, Edward Eliot, who had married his father's niece. He sat in the Tory interest and consistently supported the administration of Lord North, chiefly remarkable for its misfortunes and ineptitudes when confronted with the American revolution (see Chapter XI below).

To these events and to that policy Gibbon made no contribution, though he commented on them in his letters. Bury justly remarks that "we cannot look with much complacency on Gibbon's career as a politician", but Gibbon himself was even less complacent about it, being as free from illusions on his own character as on that of others: "After a fleeting illusive hope, prudence condemned me to acquiesce in the humble station of a mute." His gift was for conversation, not oratory. He was not in fact a House of Commons man, except in the sense of being a back-bencher, yet his talents were too remarkable to make him a congruous figure in the background. "Timidity" he wrote "was fortified by pride, and even the success of my pen discouraged the trial of my voice." (*Autobiography*, p. 178.)

That, perhaps, was the true secret of his silence. It is rarely that a man of letters succeeds in the House of Commons. Burke, of course, is the great exception. Others, such as Disraeli and Churchill, have been so richly gifted with qualities of courage no less than of intellect that it would be remarkable if they failed in any career. But the "literary mind proper", of which Gibbon was so conspicuous an example, finds too painful a contrast between the written and the spoken word, unless this is broken by the decent intervals of conversation or the discreet interjections of admirers. In writing, Gibbon composed his periods with deliberation, walking up and down the room, while in talking he had "a vein of pleasantry" which was equally remote from the vigour of oratory. "Those who have enjoyed the society of Mr. Gibbon" wrote Sheffield "will agree with me that his conversation was still more captivating than his writings." It was these gentler qualities, the friendliness of his writing, the charm of his conversation, which made him shrink from the rougher exchanges of public debate.

There remained, even after his success, a certain timidity in his character which may have arisen from the disturbances of his childhood and his submissions to his father. Some may also see in his dandyism and his extreme courtesy more evidence of timidity; in the fastidiousness of his appearance and in the anxiety to avoid offence. In him it was not an unattractive quality, for he was not one of those writers who show a contrast between the hesitations of their behaviour and the aggressiveness of their pen. He had an equal urbanity in both, and he even said that he might have softened his two chapters on Christianity, if he had foreseen their effect on "the pious, the timid, and the prudent". The remark was perhaps ironical, but those three qualities were not absent from himself, though concealed by the urbanity with which he confronted the world.

Lacking the forceful gifts to make his way in the House of Commons, he was propelled forward by his own fame as the historian of the Roman Empire and by the pressure of his friends. In 1779 he was appointed one of the Lords Commissioners of Trade and Plantations, which increased his income by over seven hundred a year without imposing any very severe tax on his leisure. In relating this fact in his memoirs he urbanely recalled Burke's attack on "the perpetual virtual adjournment, and the unbroken sitting vacation of the Board of Trade", to add that the speech was heard with delight "even by those whose existence he proscribed". He could in fact accept such an office with an easy conscience, as he was one of the very few who would have deserved support at the public expense in any age, if not from a sinecure, then from a Civil List pension. In 1780 he lost his seat at Liskeard, as his cousin Edward Eliot had joined the opposition, "and the electors of Liskeard are commonly of the same opinion as Mr. Eliot". In the following year the administration found him a seat in a by-election at Lymington in Hampshire. But a year later, with the fall of the Government, the Lords of Trade were abolished and Gibbon lost a useful addition to his income, a fact which greatly influenced him in deciding to retire to Lausanne.

In the same year as he was elected at Lymington, the second and third volumes of *The Decline and Fall* had appeared. Already he had decided to continue the work beyond the fall of the Empire in the West and to pursue through the Eastern Empire a history which was only to end with the fall of Constantinople in 1453.

The vastness of this undertaking is a sufficient explanation of the deficiencies in his political career. The best qualities of his mind had been expended not on London but on Rome.

IX

THE ROMAN EMPIRE

The rise of a city, which swelled into an empire, may deserve, as a singular prodigy, the reflection of a philosophic mind. But the decline of Rome was the natural and inevitable effect of immoderate greatness. Prosperity ripened the principle of decay; the causes of destruction multiplied with the extent of conquest; and as soon as time or accident had removed the artificial supports, the stupendous fabric yielded to the pressure of its own weight. The story of its ruin is simple and obvious; and instead of inquiring *why* the Roman empire was destroyed, we should rather be surprised that it had subsisted so long.

> "General Observations on the Fall of the Roman Empire in the West," *The Decline and Fall*, ch. xxxviii (vol. iv, p. 173).

WHEN the first volume of *The Decline and Fall* was published in 1776, it was read eagerly and rapidly. The first edition, though it had already been doubled by the foresight of the printer, was sold within a few days. "I am at a loss" Gibbon wrote in his memoirs "how to describe the success of the work, without betraying the vanity of the writer," for he had to admit: "My book was on every table, and almost on every toilette; the historian was crowned by the taste or fashion of the day." (*Autobiography*, p. 180.)

To explain this instant success, it is necessary to look beyond the merits of the work, for not every work of scholarship has appealed so immediately to the general public. It was read as happily as a novel, and indeed, as George Saintsbury wrote in *The Peace of the Augustans*, "large parts of Gibbon are a great deal more interesting, in the simplest and most guileless sense of the word, than most modern novels". Saintsbury also maintained that "Gibbon anticipated some of the best points in the historical novel—if one may not almost say that some of the best points in Scott's handling of fiction owe a little, and not so very little, to Gibbon's handling of fact".

As in a novel there were the "splendid anecdotes", to which Coleridge lightly referred, but there were also brilliant portraits of the emperors, as that of Augustus in Chapter III: "A cool head, an unfeeling heart, and a cowardly disposition, prompted him, at the age of nineteen, to assume the mask of hypocrisy, which he never afterwards laid aside." (i, p. 78.)

Or again:

> The virtue of Marcus Aurelius Antoninus was of a severer and more laborious kind. It was the well-earned harvest of many a learned conference, of many a patient lecture, and many a midnight lucubration... His meditations, composed in the tumult of a camp, are still extant; and he even condescended to give lessons of philosophy in a more public manner than was perhaps consistent with the modesty of a sage, or the dignity of an emperor.... He was severe to himself, indulgent to the imperfections of others, just and beneficent to all mankind... His memory was revered by a grateful posterity, and above a century after his death, many persons preserved the image of Marcus Antoninus, among those of their household gods.   (i, pp. 84–5.)

The golden age of Trajan and the Antonines had been preceded by an age of iron. It is almost superfluous to enumerate the unworthy successors of Augustus. Their unparalleled vices, and the splendid theatre on which they were acted, have saved them from oblivion. The dark unrelenting Tiberius, the furious Caligula, the feeble Claudius, the profligate and cruel Nero, the beastly Vitellius, and the timid inhuman Domitian, are condemned to everlasting infamy.   (i, pp. 86–7.)

"The splendid theatre on which they were acted . . ."—the setting is dramatic and the figures are sculptural, as impressive and as authentic as the busts in a museum, such as Gibbon had contemplated in Florence.

But beyond these incidental delights, the first volume, especially, had also a plot. As the reader follows the changing fortunes of Rome his sympathies are insensibly drawn to her side, so that he is alarmed by the attacks of the barbarians or by the weakness of an emperor, while his spirits rise when a great leader assumes command and the frontiers are guarded. He has the satisfaction of a child whose sand castle still stands when the tide ebbs. Yet he knows that the Empire is to fall, and he presses on with the pleasurable anguish of a detection addict to know how the crime was committed. Among Gibbon's earliest reading was Pope's *Iliad*, whose reader has the same feeling of sympathy for Hector, yet the same urge to reach the last line:

And peaceful slept the mighty Hector's shade.

There was all this for the general reader, but there was immensely more for the serious student of history and the scholar. When Gibbon wrote, history in England could record the great name of Clarendon, but more often plodded in the track of old chronicles. In Scotland, Hume and Robertson, themselves influenced by the broader sweep of French historical writing, had set the example—so well that even after *The Decline and Fall* had appeared Gibbon said that he had "never presumed" to set his name beside theirs. Yet he had surpassed these masters: sixteen years before the first publication of *The Decline and Fall*, he had himself described Hume's *History of England* as "ingenious but superficial", and it was as a philosopher more than as a historian that Hume won his esteem. This esteem was so great that he could say: "A letter from Mr. Hume overpaid the labour of ten years."

Hume had welcomed *The Decline and Fall* with these words:

> Whether I consider the dignity of your style, the depth of your matter, or the extensiveness of your learning, I must regard the work as equally the object of esteem; and I own that if I had not previously had the happiness of your personal acquaintance, such a performance from an Englishman in our age would have given me some surprise. You may smile at this sentiment, but as it seems to me that your countrymen, for almost a whole generation, have given themselves up to barbarous and absurd faction, and have totally neglected all polite letters, I no longer expected any valuable production ever to come from them.

Hume was writing from Edinburgh, the Athens of the North, where he died in the same year—"the death of a philosopher", as Gibbon observed.

Other scholars joined in attesting Gibbon's accuracy and learning. Those Christians who were affronted by his treatment of religion were more remarkable for their tempers than for their knowledge or intellect, and they foolishly tried to assail his facts, which were complete, before his sympathies, which were partial. Of his *Vindication*, composed against them,

Gibbon could only say: "A victory over such antagonists was a sufficient humiliation."

When the second and third volumes appeared in 1781, the attack was renewed by Archdeacon Travis, to whom Porson, the greatest scholar of his day, replied, and lent the weight of his authority to Gibbon's accuracy. Nor have scholars since his day shaken that testimony. Gibbon remains, as Morison wrote, "a common mine of authentic facts". A historian of Freeman's eminence could write: "That Gibbon should ever be displaced seems impossible. . . . Whatever else is read, Gibbon must be read too."

Yet these facts never clogged the stream of the narrative. What impressed readers of the first volume was the panorama it provided of the Roman Empire, much as they were impressed by an eighteenth-century landscape with its wide vistas and its eminences crowned with temples. Gibbon did not simply compile a chronicle; he revealed a vision. He was vivid. When a threat to the Empire arises, it is immediately visible, as in Chapter V, when "the capital was terrified by the strange aspect and manners of a multitude of barbarians" (i, p. 135), or a reference is made to "the Pretorian bands, whose licentious fury was the first symptom and cause of the decline of the Roman Empire". (i, p. 114.) Yet these vivid details never falsified the perspective. From the French writers of the Enlightenment Gibbon had learnt the art of generalizing, yet in the accumulation of his facts he was closer to the monumental labours of the Benedictines, whose diligence they more seldom emulated. Both observations and facts were rendered with an acuteness of criticism that was wholly his own.

The extent and the mass of his work aroused a respect which has never diminished, so that *The Decline and Fall* has become in literature a counterpart to the "Seven Wonders of the World". A royal duke was reported to have greeted the second volume with the words: "Another damned thick, square book! Always scribble, scribble, scribble! Eh! Mr. Gibbon?" Others as illiterate have been no less impressed, and even a Prime Minister increased his reputation when it was known that he had read the entire work three times before he was twenty-one. John Morley, with a wide acquaintance in the nineteenth-century House of Commons, said: "Most of the men I have known would rather have written *The Decline and Fall* than been Mr. Pitt"—evidence of Gibbon's wisdom in conserving his energies in the House.

This formidable reputation has given the work an odour of dullness with the general public which a first taste of the style may not at once dispel. Yet Gibbon remains an engaging and even an engrossing writer; after a few pages, delight in his epithets and in his wit convert the reader. Porson, in a phrase worthy of Gibbon, made the chief criticism of the style in saying that he sometimes "draws out the thread of his verbosity finer than the staple of his argument". Recurring adjectives— passions which persist in being "fierce", rocks in being "barren", successors in being "degenerate"—affect some with a similar tedium, but to others they have the charm of repetition in verse. It is a style more pleasing to modern ears than to those of the last century, when it offended writers as different as Coleridge and Mill, who, though he disliked Gibbon in other respects, admitted that his research was the only work of his age which stood up to later criticism.

Few have disputed Gibbon's literary quality or the personality of his style. Among more recent writers Mr. Quennell has observed: "Than *The Decline and Fall* there is probably no book of equal size and scope more thoroughly imbued with the characteristic quality of a single man's intelligence." Mr. G. M. Young remarks: "His picture is drawn with the integrity of a scholar, and coloured with the intention of an artist." Mr.

D. M. Low draws attention to the dramatic qualities of Gibbon's gifts: "The characters rush on and off the stage tumultuously."

The unity, the art, and the dramatic qualities of *The Decline and Fall* are evident to all sensitive critics, but the ordinary reader may be more drawn by its serenity. It has the calm and the proportion of a great temple, and as architecture is the art most impressive and most accessible to the ordinary man, so the ordinary reader is better able to appreciate Gibbon than works of similar scholarship in which the material has been less skilfully disposed.

The material itself was of universal interest—"The Roman Empire" as Stevenson wrote "under whose toppling monuments we were all cradled." It was of interest to all, but to none more than the readers of the eighteenth century, when Members of Parliament regarded themselves as "senators", and even the revolutionaries of France gave themselves nicknames drawn from the history of Rome. Rome was closer to them than to us, but Gibbon brought it even closer to them because he bridged the formidable gap between the last days of the Republic and the emergence of modern states.

"On the continuity of the Roman Empire" wrote Bury "depended the unity of Gibbon's work." There was unity in the work, but it was far from equal, as Bury himself was the first to insist. It is permissible to doubt whether Gibbon ever recaptured the felicity of the first volume. He was happiest there because it included the age in which the human race was "most happy and prosperous". It was the most dramatic period of his history because there was still the hope of saving the Rome he loved, before the triumph of the barbarians who became, as he later recalled in Chapter XXXVI in a phrase that resumed the whole history, "the servants, the allies, and at length the masters, of the Romans". (iv, p. 58.)

When the second and third volumes appeared, there were
readers who found the narrative less absorbing. "An author
who cannot ascend will always appear to sink" was Gibbon's
comment, but while it was true that he could hardly ascend
above the supreme level of the first volume, it can also be
maintained that there is a decline throughout the whole work,
consistent with the decline of the empire he was recording;
not a decline in scholarship, nor in style, nor in skill, but in
interest. He was too fondly attached to Rome to write of
her ruin with the same love as he wrote of her defence.
There is a revealing sentence in Chapter XLIV, when he
retraced his steps to treat the subject of Roman law: "Attached
to no party, interested only for the truth and candour of
history . . . although I have devoted myself to writing the
annals of a declining monarchy, I shall embrace the occasion
to breathe the pure and invigorating air of the republic."
(iv, p. 471.) His sympathies were with a Rome which, still vivid
in his first volume, progressively declined as he wrote of it,
and not even his great gifts could maintain the same intensity
of interest. In the second and third volumes there is still
animation, but the last three volumes on the Eastern Empire
were altogether inferior in inspiration, because the sympathy
had declined with the fall of the Western Empire. So, increasingly, sympathy was replaced with disdain.

The question of sympathy is closely relevant to the two
famous Chapters XV and XVI on Christianity. They were
written with all the sympathy for Rome which informed his
first volume, and they were written from the standpoint of
Rome, because Gibbon was convinced, as he wrote in his
Autobiography (p. 172), that "the propagation of the Gospel,
and the triumph of the Church, are inseparably connected
with the decline of the Roman monarchy". Few would dispute that statement of fact, but opinions may vary widely as

to how far they were cause and effect. Gibbon himself was moderate on this point. In his "General Observations" at the end of the third volume he only said that "the introduction, or at least the abuse, of Christianity had some influence on the decline and fall of the Roman Empire". He even said: "If the decline of the Roman Empire was hastened by the conversion of Constantine, his victorious religion broke the violence of the fall, and mollified the ferocious temper of the conquerors." (iv, p. 175.) When at the conclusion of the whole work he composed his famous phrase "I have described the triumph of barbarism and religion" (vii, p. 321), he was still stating an evident fact, for none could deny that the two had risen together out of the ruins of the Roman Empire.

Yet that phrase deserves its fame, for it is a perfect embodiment of Gibbon's attitude. Obviously it was written in malice, but no less obviously in complete accord with "the truth and candour of history". Truth and malice may sometimes be united, as when Pilate wrote "Jesus of Nazareth, the King of the Jews". Gibbon, no less Roman than Pilate, washed his hands in the blood of the martyrs. He was a humane man, and he would have preferred that they had not suffered, but he was more concerned to point out the breadth and justice of the Roman administration than to admire their virtues, which to his mind had already been magnified to the prejudice of truth. He wrote from the angle of a Roman official, and he relied on Roman sources, yet he was not uncritical in his use of them, for in Chapter XV he observed that "this unfavourable picture, though not devoid of a faint resemblance, betrays, by its dark colouring and distorted features, the pencil of an enemy". (ii, p. 70.)

Some have maintained that his own picture suffers from those defects, but it would be inexact to apply this phrase to it, for what was most evident to Christians in his own day and since was precisely its lack of colour. It appeared distorted because it was drawn in a different perspective. So a Chinese historian, with a respect for civil government, might have written of the barbarous superstitions which impeded its administration. As the average Roman official had as little regard for Christianity, Gibbon has given a valid account of Christian development from that point of view.

Yet it would be idle to pretend that he adopted this attitude simply as a historian, or as a modern historical novelist revives a distant period in an effort of imaginative sympathy. He was protesting with bland irony against the generations of Christian chroniclers who had failed to distinguish between legend and history, and who had used their prejudices to whiten all their friends and to blacken all their enemies. In redressing the balance he was inevitably placed in the position of a devil's advocate.

A devil's advocate is always a useful official, an indispensible figure in the process of canonization, but no less useful in registering a protest against the sanctification of the past. He has become a necessary ghost hovering in the mind of every modern historian, to warn him against the danger of partisan sympathies—so much so that it was Bury, the author of *A History of the Freedom of Thought*, who in editing Gibbon warned the reader against the religious chapters in *The Decline and Fall*.

Whether it is really possible to hold the balance between two conflicting spirits, and to write as a disembodied spirit oneself, is more doubtful. Justice itself demands that a historian should correct the distortions of his predecessors, and in so doing he is likely to make others of his own. He too becomes a devil's advocate, and the court of history turns again to the champions of the saint. When Gibbon enquired in Chapter XV: "In the long series of ecclesiastical history, does there exist a single instance of a saint asserting that he himself possessed the gift of miracles?" (ii, p. 32n) he raised a question which either side might have advanced as their own; and when in Chapter LIX he wrote that St. Bernard "seems to have preserved as much reason and humanity as may be reconciled with the character of a saint" (vi, p. 346), he was hardly less ambiguous. But this was constantly his tone, for his irony was often no more than a shrug masking his deep uncertainty about human motives, a quality which will be more fully treated in the following chapter.

What is more certain is that, at the time when it was published, *The Decline and Fall* was even more useful to Christians than to sceptics in arousing them from the lethargy into which they had fallen, and in revealing to them past sins which they had been too ready to accept as virtues. Joseph Butler's *Analogy of Religion*, the greatest Christian apologetic of the eighteenth century and perhaps of English literature, had been received with much the same bewilderment, when it appeared exactly forty years before Gibbon's first volume, because it too broke through the conventions of controversy. Butler had been writing against the deists, and Gibbon's Chapter XV on the origins of Christianity had been written from a deist point of view, but both men opened the same "Chinese" perspective on a familiar world, and caused a similar shock.

Yet there is little reason to doubt that Gibbon, as a deist, was hardly less shocked by the liberties which Christians had taken with his Supreme Being, the Author of Nature, than they were by the liberties he took with their religion. He regarded miracles as conjuring tricks unworthy of so Supreme a Being. It was the Incarnation, with all that followed from it of divine intervention and presence in the world, that offended his puritan creed. This repugnance was strengthened by an aristocratic distaste for popular religion. "A state of scepticism" he wrote in Chapter XV "may amuse a few inquisitive minds. But the practice of superstition is so congenial to the multitude that, if they are forcibly awakened, they still regret the loss of their pleasing vision." (ii, p. 59.) The same distaste is evident in Chapter XXVIII where he wrote: " . . . the smoke of incense, the perfume of flowers, and the glare of lamps and tapers . . . edifying pictures, which could not long escape the abuse of indiscreet or idolatrous devotion, represented the image, the attributes, and the miracles of the tutelar saint." (iii, pp. 225–6.)

Behind his irony and his scepticism, there sometimes emerge the more austere features of the aristocratic and disapproving deist, disdaining no less than a Mohammedan the idolatry of the Christian dogs, as in Chapter XL when he wrote that "the enthusiast who entered the dome of St. Sophia might be tempted to suppose that it was the residence, or even the workmanship, of the Deity. Yet how dull is the artifice, how insignificant is the labour, if it be compared with the formation of the vilest insect that crawls upon the surface of the temple!" (iv, p. 264.) This is an unusual passage in Gibbon, with its strange echo of "Solomon in all his glory was not arrayed like one of these". Some have questioned whether he was a deist or a deeper sceptic, though in that age not everybody distinguished between deists and freethinkers, so fine was the distinction between them; but in this passage at least there is the religious tone of a believer in the Author of Nature.

It was the deist who predominated over the Roman official when he wrote Chapter XV, "to inquire by what means the Christian faith obtained so remarkable a victory" and conceded that one answer was "the ruling providence of its great Author", though it was with an ironical affectation of humility that he only presumed to consider "the secondary causes of the rapid growth of the Christian church" (ii, p. 2).

His examination of these secondary causes was executed with candour, but it is in the distinction between the primary and secondary causes that he separated himself from Christians, for whom the primary cause, the Incarnation itself, is so overwhelmingly more important than any secondary issues. Yet even in the treatment of his five secondary causes, in two of them Gibbon was influenced, not by his own opinions, which he knew and balanced with the faithful impartiality of the great historical conscience that he had, but by his own view of human motives, which was concealed from him in the way that every man's character is hidden from himself. Of the doctrine of a future life, he wrote: "When the promise of eternal happiness was proposed to mankind on condition of adopting the faith, and of observing the precepts of the Gospel, it is no wonder that so advantageous an offer should have been accepted by great numbers of every religion, of every rank, and of every province in the Roman Empire." (ii, p. 24.) Only a man with a disdainful view of mankind's credulity would assume that men and women might accept such a promise with little regard for its evidence or its truth. Something of the same limitation appears when Gibbon treats of "the pure and austere morals of the Christians", which he ascribes largely to their care for their reputations. That was perhaps a motive which weighed more with the sociable and sensitive Gibbon than it does with the majority of men, and self-respect of that sort is probably more widespread in Anglo-Saxon societies than it was among the more southern, Latin, or oriental peoples of the Roman Empire.

But the chief weakness of Chapter XV is that no part is assigned in it to the love of God, which today is more often recognized as a motive in mankind even by those who regard it as an illusion. Gibbon recognized it to dismiss religion as superstition, but it is a limitation in him as a historian that in confining religion to that one category he allowed himself no room to distinguish between the grossest idolatry and the practices of a St. Augustine or a St. Bernard, which, independent of an observer's opinion, are evidently different.

In Chapter XVI, which treats of the persecution of the Christians, he wrote less as a deist anxious to discount the miraculous than as a Roman official concerned to display the humanity and justice of the imperial administration. From that point of view the martyrs had only themselves to blame for their deaths. Gibbon has been criticized for the inhumanity of this view, yet it was precisely from a humane standpoint that he was writing, for the trend of his argument is that the Christians were provided with many opportunities to escape, and he sincerely lamented that they did not avail themselves of them—although he maliciously adds that many of them did.

From his own point of view and his love of Rome, he was clearly right: the Roman administration, in its treatment of Christians, compares favourably with one or two of which mankind has more recent experience. But in his urbane narrative of the persecutions, though he mentions in passing "the well-known observation" that the blood of the martyrs was the seed of the Church, he gives so little weight to this that it has no place where it really belongs—at the head of his secondary causes responsible for the growth of Christianity.

In treating of the persecutions, he was perhaps justifiably misled by his wish to point out that Christian princes, such as Charles V and Louis XIV, had persecuted even more ignobly. Yet these had the same effect, just as the fires of Smithfield were no less the seed of English Protestant churches. But Gibbon was no more indulgent to Protestants—"a creed of daring fanatics"—than to other Christians, and his two chapters on Christianity may have given more offence to them than to Catholics, so constantly does he identify the early Christians with all the practices of the Roman Church, for in this the French sceptic in him and the Roman official shared the same view, that of Christianity as "a singular but an inoffensive mode of faith and worship". (ii, p. 76.)

This pleasant phrase, which occurs at the beginning of Chapter XVI, brings out the lack of seriousness in Gibbon's treatment of religion. But it is thrown into sharper relief when he writes of Athanasius, of whom, it is generally agreed, he gives a striking portrait. Newman even maintained that "Athanasius stands out more grandly in Gibbon than in the pages of the orthodox ecclesiastical historians". Certainly Gibbon deals nobly with Athanasius and even refrains from jest when he takes shelter with a woman, yet the best that he can find to say of him in Chapter XXI is that "Athanasius displayed a superiority of character and abilities which would have qualified him, far better than the degenerate sons of Constantine, for the government of a great monarchy". (ii, p. 384.)

It is a notable and a generous tribute, but it is no less remarkable that the highest praise for a saint should be that he was worthy to occupy the place of a politician. Gibbon was serious about government, and the religious figures who won his respect were not the thinkers, nor the contemplatives, but the administrators. In Chapter XXVII he praised St. Ambrose, not for his saintly qualities, but because he wisely ruled his people of Milan and "acted from the laudable persuasion that every measure of civil government may have some connection with the glory of God and the interest of true religion". (iii, p. 183.)

Sometimes Gibbon's administrative outlook enabled him to see through the haze of religious controversy to an underlying motive, as in Chapter XXI, when he remarked of the riots in Constantinople that "the writer who should impute these tumults solely to a religious principle would betray a very imperfect knowledge of human nature" (ii, p. 108), but he was as apt to diminish motives more respectably inspired. For his eyes were constantly fixed on the Roman Government and the "great republic" of Europe which inherited its traditions: it is significant that his grandest tribute to the Christian Church, in Chapter XXXVII, when he was coming to the end of the Empire in the West, was more truly a vindication of these principles:

> The perpetual correspondence of the Latin clergy, the frequent pilgrimages to Rome and Jerusalem, and the growing authority of the popes, cemented the union of the Christian republic, and gradually produced the similar manners, and common jurisprudence, which have distinguished from the rest of mankind the independent, and even hostile nations of modern Europe.
>
> (iv, pp. 86–7.)

Yet there are passages in *The Decline and Fall* when Gibbon's own character and experience gave him a peculiar insight even in religious matters. His portrayal of the Emperor Julian is an equal masterpiece of sympathy and of criticism. In his *Autobiography* Gibbon noted with satisfaction that "my impartial balance of the virtues and vices of Julian was generally praised". (p. 192.) Since then Julian has often been regarded as Gibbon's chosen hero, yet if he enjoyed an advantage in understanding Julian, he wrote of him with as little illusion as of himself.

Like Gibbon, Julian had renounced Christianity and devoted himself instead to the Roman Empire. "But the young prince" wrote Gibbon in Chapter XXIII "who aspired to the glory of a hero rather than a martyr, consulted his safety by dissembling his religion." The result was to increase his distaste for Christianity: "But as every act of dissimulation must be painful to an ingenuous spirit, the profession of Christianity increased the aversion of Julian for a religion which oppressed the freedom of the mind." (ii, p. 467.)

Yet Julian was also sincerely devoted to the gods, who might have had more understanding from Gibbon if he had been a Christian; and when he was able to restore their worship, he forfeited a measure of sympathy from Gibbon, who then referred to "the ruling passions of his soul, superstition and vanity". (ii, p. 476.) Yet in the following chapter, when Julian died a hero on the confines of the Empire, this phrase is strangely altered into "the love of virtue and of fame, which had been the ruling passions of his life". (ii, p. 544.) Both phrases had their truth, but the change is interesting in its revelation of Gibbon's emotions. Finally after Julian's funeral, Gibbon pronounced judgment:

> His various character and singular manners afforded an ample scope for pleasantry and ridicule. In the exercise of his uncommon talents, he often descended below the majesty of his rank. Alexander was transformed into Diogenes; the philosopher was degraded into a priest.
>
> (ii, p. 558.)

It is difficult to avoid seeing, in Gibbon's long and careful treatment of Julian, the main theme of *The Decline and Fall*, for he had fought equally against the "barbarism and religion" whose triumph Gibbon noted at the end of his work. From Julian's death, they both continued their advance, and no other emperor was to fight with equal valour against both. Though, even when he turned to the Eastern Empire, Gibbon always wrote greatly of a great man, such as Belisarius, he never again had so congenial a subject. Julian is in a sense the tragic hero of *The Decline and Fall*, in his noble and hopeless battle against new forces which were to transform the lands of the Empire—and Gibbon shared that tragedy, in that he had to advance through a thousand years of Christianity without any sympathy for the motives which led men to embrace it. For if he was supreme in his evocation of great events and great men, there was always in his mind a doubt as to the motives which inspired them, even in their least religious acts.

X

DUBIOUS MOTIVES

That I am equal or superior to some of these, the effects of modesty or affectation cannot force me to dissemble.

(*Autobiography*, p. 5.)

IN the first pages of his *Autobiography*, Gibbon referred briefly to previous models of the art, pointing out that "it would not be difficult to produce a long list of ancients and moderns who, in various forms, have exhibited their own portraits. Such portraits are often the most interesting, and sometimes the only interesting parts of their writings. . . ." After mentioning a few names, some great, others more obscure, he made the remark quoted above, balancing modesty against affectation.

Such remarks occur frequently both in the *Autobiography* and in *The Decline and Fall*. This means of striking a balance is natural enough to the impartial historian, who has constantly to be comparing one text with another, deciding between conflicting authorities, judging whether a man is the hero claimed by his own party or the villain asserted by his enemies. These points emerge particularly in the early centuries with which *The Decline and Fall* first deals, as there is a constant contrast between the old Roman and the new Christian writers, who differed most sharply on their view of Julian as a great emperor or a great apostate.

In his portrait of Julian, Gibbon struck a masterly balance. It is his greatness as a historian that he so skilfully achieved a balance, in spite of the vast bulk of the authorities whom he had to reconcile; and the smoothness of his narrative, which is the greatest joy to his readers, proves how well he reduced them to a coherent whole.

What is almost more remarkable, he achieved the same balance in his own character, for there is no clear distinction between Gibbon the historian and Gibbon the man—the same serenity marked his life and his history, the same amusement enlivened his conversation and his written pages. The surface was always calm. As there are no gargoyles in an eighteenth-century structure, no irregularities in an eighteenth-century landscape, so there are no obstacles in Gibbon's own stream.

This serenity is so wonderful to more troubled minds that it may appear more proper to the gods, who have their Olympian calm only because, remote on Mount Olympus, they are indifferent to the joys and miseries of mankind, at whom

> . . . the bolts are hurled
> Far below them in the valleys, and the clouds are lightly
> curled
> Round their golden houses, girdled with the gleaming
> world. . .

Gibbon surveyed life with this Olympian calm, and in raising himself above the general level of mankind he was obliged to occupy the platform of the gods in whom he did not believe, which left him alone on his eminence. It is the fate of sceptics that, however sincere their charity towards mankind, their aloofness makes them aristocrats, because the majority of mankind have always accorded some piety to the divine, however general scepticism may be in a particular period of history. Sceptics charge religion with persecution, which is a crime against man's free will, but themselves often show as little respect for the divine heart of his personality, which is a crime against the dead no less than against the living. They may have a warm sympathy with the sufferings of mankind, and a hatred for cruelty, but their aristocratic position makes them indifferent towards many of the common feelings of humanity.

Gibbon had this sort of superiority, which increased the coldness of his Olympian calm. At times this coldness, natural to the heights, has the chill which mystics have always associated with the presence of evil. He was very characteristic of his age, and this same chill passed like a draught through many great corridors of the eighteenth century. It is present in the boredom and indifference of Versailles. Sometimes it gives a shiver even to the supreme artistry of Pope. The genius and the laughter of Swift cannot quite escape the whistle of its bitterness. The same shudder is caused when Horace Walpole records bland amusement at public executions. Boswell's temperament was not of his age, but incidents in his journals produce a similar chill which freezes sympathy for his vanities and uncertainties. Perhaps Johnson was more immune, but there is a chill in his constant fear of the grave, and the "great Bear" was a creature of the cold.

This is enough to indicate that the chill was not confined to sceptics, and there were some among them with warmth enough to escape it. No doubt it was partly due to the artificiality of the age. It was present in Sterne, whom Saintsbury called the most artificial of all writers. It was most marked among the aristocracy of England and France, in the aloofness of their disdain and in the coldness of their pleasures. Perhaps it was an aftermath to the passionate political and religious debates of the preceding century.

Certainly it was the chill of a civilized indifference, for it did not extend to the more passionate climate of Scotland. The

Jacobites were able to advance so far into England, not only through English indifference, but owing to their own fervour. There was a geniality even in the scepticism of Hume, and it was from Scotland that the return to warm human emotion was announced in the poetry of Burns.

Naturally it was this eighteenth-century coldness which prompted the Romantic reaction, which also produced a religious revival. This connection between emotion and religion is further emphasized by the fact that one great eighteenth-century figure to escape the chill was John Wesley. Evidently it required a saint to withstand the bitterness of that cold.

The artistocratic chill was so strong that in the following century, where it was admired in the "iron" qualities of Wellington, it remained an aspect of the English character, in marked contrast to the singing, dancing, and music-making which had still been considered typically English in the early seventeenth century. But it remained an aristocratic trait, though aped by those below. There were other more human influences at work, not only in Romantic and religious re-vivalism, but in the gustier characters of a Fielding, a Cobbett, a Dickens.

Gibbon read and admired Fielding, finding *Tom Jones* an "exquisite picture of human manners", but recalling that the author was "of the younger branch of the Earls of Denbigh" (*Autobiography*, p. 3). Yet it hardly requires that touch to reveal how far Gibbon was from the warmth of Fielding. The chill of the eighteenth century is nowhere more evident than in the life and in the pages of Gibbon.

No Englishman was more characteristic of the Enlightenment, which had its own bleakness; for the original aim of the movement was to re-examine the whole field of human knowledge in a critical spirit, discounting the prejudices of legend or piety and the poetic myths in which men had embodied their memories of the earth or their aspirations towards heaven. The value of this enlightened approach is obvious enough to the discovery of truth in many fields, but it is hardly less evident that it contributed an element to the chill of the age. The Enlightenment was eminently a movement of criticism. It is as a critic, more than a scholar, that Bayle is remembered, while the shortcomings of Voltaire's scholarship shocked Gibbon himself.

As a scholar Gibbon was possibly the finest product of the Enlightenment, but as a critic he was no less representative of the movement's tendency to ignore the deeper psychological and human truths. One illustration of this aspect in the Enlightenment is that Rousseau, who prepared the ground for so many later developments in psychology, stood outside it. Critical, no less than personal, reasons set Gibbon against him.

Religious scepticism itself implies a degree of isolation from the common life of mankind, but the scepticism of the eighteenth century, so marked in Gibbon, extended to the general motives and fate of humanity. There is a revealing passage in his *Journal* (23 October 1762):

> Indeed, I believe it happens throughout, that our most important actions have been often determined by chance, caprice, or some very inadequate motive.

The proper detachment of the historian was reinforced by a deeper uncertainty about human motives. Both the smoothness of his prose and the serenity of his mind owed much to the indifference with which he presented two contradictory motives, such as modesty or affectation, and refrained from deciding between them. Some of these remarks were made in a spirit of irony, some with a shrug, some in genuine uncertainty.

When in Chapter LIX of *The Decline and Fall*, writing of St. Bernard and Clairvaux, he asserted that "it is impossible for us to ascertain the separate shares of accident, or fancy, of imposture, and of fiction" (vi, p. 348), it was perhaps indifference that predominated. But there are other passages which display a deeper uncertainty.

Typical examples occur in Chapter XLVII of *The Decline and Fall*, which concerns controversies on the Incarnation. First comes a light reference to "absurd or impious conclusions". (v, p. 113.) Then, in treating of Cyril of Alexandria, Gibbon declares that "his friends were stationed to lead or second the applause of the congregation". (v, p. 115.) On the following page occurs "a malicious or accidental tumult".

Such imputations are comparatively unimportant, but the same uncertainty prevails when Gibbon is more aroused. He states that "the murder of Hypatia has imprinted an indelible stain on the character and religion of Cyril of Alexandria", but in introducing the subject and in according the blame he says no more than that "he soon prompted, or accepted, the sacrifice of a virgin". (v, p. 117.) The smoothness of the narrative alone conceals the fatal nature of the alternative.

The same uncertainty is revealed when he refers to the Churches of Persia, which were "distinguished by a liberal principle of reason, or at least of policy" (v, p. 157), or when "the unsuccessful competitors of Nestorius indulged their pious or personal resentment". (v, p. 120.) The difference, not always trivial, is glossed over by the smile, as when "whatever is superstitious or absurd, might claim the protection of the monks", on the same page. As Gibbon usually equates religion with superstition, the reader is left with the impression that religion is absurd, but the very lightness with which the suggestion is made implies an indifference or uncertainty about the motives of remote people, more than any desire to challenge them. Yet in his *Autobiography* (p. 45), Gibbon declared: "From my childhood I had been fond of religious disputation." Evidently he had lost interest, yet still allowed his own doubts to colour the past, as when the followers of Photius display their "zeal to erase the suspicion, or to expiate the guilt of idolatry". (v, p. 144.) A synod is treated "with sincere or affected reverence". Then comes a very striking case: "The bounteous alms of John the eleemosynary were dictated by superstition, or benevolence, or policy". (v, p. 172.) It is an extreme instance, for it so covers the possible motives of John's generosity as to leave them hardly less in the dark than if they had not been mentioned. Yet even here a point is made, for the reader is left with the impression that John's motives were mixed, if not dubious.

Gibbon was far from being alone in ascribing mixed motives to mankind, nor is such a view confined to cynics, but his doubts were more acute than those of most men. There is a distinction in the English language between saying that motives are doubtful and suggesting that they are dubious—which is more often the effect of Gibbon's remarks. It is his use of such phrases which has brought upon him the charge of employing innuendo to discredit religion; but more often it is not religion, but human nature, that is the victim, for his use of the device was general and impartial. That his doubts over motives went deep is proved by the fact that he was no less ready to question his own, as in the "modesty or affectation" with which he compared his *Autobiography* to others, or in the same work when he wrote that he was "too modest, or too proud, to rate my own value by that of my associates". (p. 202.) Such references to modesty were not only ironical, for his dislike of hypocrisy and self-deception inspired him in the effort to eliminate them from his own character, yet never satisfied him that he had succeeded. To escape them, he was careful to avoid all high-flown sentiments. As he wrote in his memoirs: "My temper is not very susceptible of enthusiasm, and the enthusiasm which I do not feel I have ever scorned to affect." (p. 157.) It was logical, though unjust, that he should scorn it in others who were more susceptible to it. "His work was written" says Sir A. W. Ward "not only without enthusiasm, but with a conscious distrust, which his age shared to the full, of enthusiasts."

But it was not only enthusiasts whose motives he doubted. Impartially he viewed the characters of history, repeatedly leaving it an open question whether their motives were patriotism or vanity, valour or ignorance, honour or superstition, policy or humanity. It is natural enough, in the world of Gibbon, that men should enjoy the "real or imaginary comforts of religious worship", but it is less evident, on an occasion of rape, why it should be the "willing or reluctant maid" who is ravished. Speculation on a woman's attachment to her virtue in a distant period might seem superfluous to an historical narrative.

Here it is difficult not to refer Gibbon's doubts on the virtue of religion and of women to the events of his youth, when he had to examine his own motives in the affairs of Popery and of Suzanne. It is possible that his submission in both these affairs to the wishes of his father, followed by the years of subordination which prevented him from beginning work on *The Decline and Fall*, left him with doubts which gradually coloured his whole mind. It is not uncommon that a son's inferiority to his father produces a loss of confidence, and it sometimes happens that this is later resolved in an act of self-assertion or in the creation of a great work. Gibbon achieved this, but that work, in its lucidity and in its smoothness, was the fruit of the same sacrifices as had enabled him to reach serenity in his own life. In it he dismissed the deeper issues, smiling ironically at the religious debates which had occupied the greatest minds over the centuries, showing a bland amusement at their more human passions, avoiding the tensions of divine and human love as he had eluded them in his own life.

From this resulted the admirable eighteenth-century calm of his prose, but the cost at which it was bought takes something from the achievement. Serenity is not difficult to reach if the deeper tensions are kept out of sight. It is this absence of the stronger emotions which makes Gibbon so supremely characteristic of the eighteenth century's coldness. At times his uncertainty over motives afflicts his prose with deadness, because he had removed from it those elements which for many men are the only hopes and satisfactions of life.

The uncertainties of his youth are a possible explanation of his balancing of motives, but some of the alternatives with which he amuses his readers are no more than an ironical play of the intelligence, as when he writes in his memoirs of doctors summoned in childhood "to torture or relieve me", or in a later note on his health, when he spoke of his freedom from "real or imaginary ills". There is the same irony in a remark on his stay in Paris: "Among the men of letters whom I saw, d'Alembert and Diderot held the foremost rank in merit, or at least in fame." (*Autobiography*, p. 128.)

Yet even here there is evidence of a certain reluctance to commit himself, which he said was a fruit of experience: "The experience of the world inculcates a discreet reserve on the subject of our person and estate, and we soon learn that a free disclosure of our riches or poverty would provoke the malice of envy, or encourage the insolence of contempt." (*Autobiography*, p. 187.) He displayed the same caution when he abandoned the practice of reading a manuscript to his friends: "Of such friends some will praise from politeness, and some will criticize from vanity." (*Autobiography*, p. 177.) The motives ascribed are not always unworthy ones, but the truth —in this case a just estimate of his work—usually disappears between them, as in the ambiguity of the lover's sigh and the son's obedience, which draws so discreet a veil over the conflict.

Undoubtedly the effect of this balancing is one of serenity and smoothness, but like other virtues they are achieved by a sacrifice. What is most often sacrificed here is the genuine splendour and misery of the human heart, only faintly visible beneath the placid surface. Serenity requires a breadth of mind, but while today we are more accustomed to the sort of historian who, in treating of a controversy or a civil war, argues that both parties were equally right, Gibbon was more apt to maintain that both parties were equally wrong, as in his treatment of the Reformation, where, as Mr. Christopher Dawson has said, "he contrives to inflict the maximum of damage on both parties".

Similarly, in his reference to the '45 in his memoirs, he dismisses both sides with impartial disdain:

In the year 1745, the throne and the constitution were attacked by a rebellion, which does not reflect much honour on the national spirit: since the English friends of the Pretender wanted courage to join his standard, and his enemies (the bulk of the people) allowed him to advance into the heart of the kingdom. Without daring, perhaps without desiring, to aid the rebels, my father invariably adhered to the Tory opposition. (*Autobiography*, p. 20.)

The concluding doubt on his father's behaviour adds a characteristic ambiguity.

DUBIOUS MOTIVES

In all his uncertainty on human motives, Gibbon maintained the judicious tone of a man of the eighteenth-century world. His scholarship, his scepticism, his air of aristocratic aloofness, all gave the impression that he was on a serene level above the conflict of human life. But he was not really above the conflict; he had simply avoided it. Even when malice is most evident in his pages, on some female or clerical topic, he more often introduces a doubt than he provides an argument. In this he irritated and baffled Christian apologists with some success, for he left them nothing to refute—as Paley said, it is not possible to refute a sneer. He had withdrawn, both in his life and in his work, to a position where it little mattered whether the deeper passions were "real or imaginary", for they were too remote. It was characteristic of him that in eight years in the House of Commons he should never have raised his voice in public debate, which demands the assertion of principle and the voice of certainty.

Motives might be dubious, but results were palpable, and perhaps he had chosen the Roman Empire as his subject because it represented the one thing he never doubted—the force of civilization, dominating the uncertain passions of men.

XI

THE AMERICAN REVOLUTION

America is too great a subject.

(Gibbon, Letter of 29 June 1775.)

IT is an ironical fact, and one on which Gibbon was the first to comment, that the years which he devoted to the decline of the Roman Empire in the West were also those in which the British Empire lost the greatest of its provinces, also in the West. Yet history did not repeat itself: when Britain, the most western province of the Roman Empire, was abandoned in the fifth century, the British regretted the withdrawal of the legions and the interests of Rome, but the Americans triumphed by their own efforts and in their own interests, though like their allies the French, heirs of the Roman traditions of Gaul, they retained the culture and dialect of the empire from which they had broken.

The nine years of Gibbon's life between 1774, when he entered Parliament at the age of thirty-seven, and 1783, when he left England for Lausanne—also the year in which a treaty of peace was at last signed between the British and the Americans—were indeed marked for him not only by these great events, but by the publication of the first three volumes of *The Decline and Fall* and the round of Parliament, clubs, and London society. They were certainly the fullest years of his life, but their intensity stimulated him, as he noted in his memoirs: "Shall I add, that I never found my mind more vigorous, nor my composition more happy, than in the winter hurry of society and parliament?" (*Autobiography*, p. 185.)

It was true that his parliamentary duties did not weigh very heavily on him:

> I took my seat at the beginning of the memorable contest between Great Britain and America, and supported, with a sincere and silent vote, the rights, though not, perhaps, the interest, of the mother-country. (p. 178.)

This misgiving may be the note of a later wisdom, yet there are passages in *The Decline and Fall* which reflect his awareness of America's importance, and his references to the subject in his letters are among the most interesting in his whole correspondence, as they show the pressure of events upon his opinions. Nor was he unaware of the force and logic of the Whig opposition, as he refers in his memoirs to "the argumentative vehemence of Fox, who, in the conduct of a party, approved himself equal to the conduct of an empire. By such men every operation of peace and war, every principle of justice or policy, every question of authority and freedom, was attacked and defended; and the subject of the momentous contest was the union or separation of Great Britain and America." (p. 179.)

His first note of apprehension was in a letter at the end of January 1775, nine weeks before the first shot was fired at Lexington: "We are plunging every day deeper into the great business of America." In another letter at the same time he used an even stronger expression: "We are now arrived at the decisive moment of preserving or of losing for ever both our Trade and Empire." That showed remarkable foresight before the war had even begun: it was certainly the verdict of an historian, as it may one day be the verdict of history, but it is all the more surprising coming from a consistent supporter of Lord North's administration. That he could be so prescient, yet so silent in public debate, argues a singular gap between the historian and the politician, one that perhaps explains why he was not more active in the House. His judicious balancing of motives was not the best gift for a statesman faced with daily decisions. He was also too deep in his own work to give his whole mind to affairs on the other side of the Atlantic, which had never known the authority of Rome.

In the middle of May 1775, before more disquieting news had come from America, he wrote: "In this season and on America the Archangel Gabriel would not be heard . . . for myself having supported the British I must destroy the Roman Empire." By the end of May, he had found a consoling argument: " . . . unless Fanaticism gets the better of self-preservation they must soon disperse, as it is the season for sowing their Indian corn, the chief sustenance of New England." It may be here that his opinions clouded his judgment, for he was slow to admit that revolutionaries, even more than other men, do not live by bread alone.

In the first week of June 1775, he wrote of *The Decline and Fall* that "the subject is curious", and there is more than one passage in which he returns to the analogy of the two empires in decline, as if it was simply as an historian that he was witnessing both events.

Yet by a singular coincidence—remembering the length of time for a sailing-ship to cross the Atlantic with news of defeat—it was on the 17th June, the very day on which Bunker Hill was fought, that he wrote of America: "The boldest tremble, the most vigorous talk of peace."

In the following month he wrote, to his friend Holroyd, who was a Whig: " . . . nor is it so small a work as you imagine to destroy a great Empire". For the parallel between the two empires continued to impress him, and it was a noteworthy curiosity that it took the Americans much the same time to defeat the British Empire as it took him simply to describe the downfall of the Roman Empire in the West.

By the beginning of August he was properly aware of the gravity in the situation and wrote that "Scotch highlanders, Irish papists, Hanoverians, Canadians, Indians etc. will all in various shapes be employed." Ten weeks later there was an odd proposal to hire Russian troops, and Gibbon expressed the view that "the Russian general should be absolutely under the command of the British". Two days later, he was more gravely writing that "we shall find ourselves engaged in carrying on the most serious business, perhaps, that the Empire has ever known. A dark cloud still hangs over it, and though it may be necessary to proceed, the contest will be difficult, the event doubtful, and the consequence destruction".

At the beginning of the fateful year 1776, following the heavy fighting in which the Americans were repulsed from Quebec, Gibbon admitted: "The Provincials have everywhere displayed courage and abilities worthy of a better cause."

When the news that the Declaration of Independence had been signed on July 4th reached England, Gibbon wrote in the middle of August: "A tough business indeed, you see by their declaration that they have now passed the Rubicon and rendered the work of a treaty infinitely more difficult." In fact seven years were to elapse before the treaty was made.

In the spring of 1777, after his fortieth birthday, Gibbon visited Paris, where his reputation had preceded him. He was fêted by the Neckers, and a French hostess wrote that "Mr. Gibbon has the greatest success here; it is quite a struggle to get him". But even in travelling he was not allowed to forget the American revolution, as he had apprehensions of an American privateer "with a commission from Dr. Franklin" which had attacked the Harwich boat.

By the autumn he was more critical of the conduct of affairs: "What a wretched piece of work do we seem to be making of it in America." He even suggested that the French might be induced to support the British "as the weaker party". By December, following Burgoyne's excursion from Canada and his surrender at Saratoga, Gibbon reported that there was "a universal desire of peace even on the most humble conditions".

In the spring of 1778 he could even add that "we are reduced to the humiliation of suing for peace, and I much fear that we shall have the additional humiliation of being rejected". In the summer of the same year France and Spain gave their support to the Americans, which led to the British government employing Gibbon to compose in French a *Mémoire justificatif* which was delivered in 1779 as a State paper to the courts of Europe. In this he declared that "the King does not pretend to exercise a tyrannical reign over all the seas", but complained that the French encouraged American smuggling, and "the alliance of France with the revolted colonies of America had been a manifest infraction of the peace".

In this memoir he adapted his pen to the policy he ascribed to Justinian before the invasion of Africa in Chapter XLI of *The Decline and Fall*, when "the war was preceded, according to the practice of civilised nations, by the most solemn protestations, that each party was sincerely desirous of peace". (iv, p. 290.)

In the same year, returning to his proper work, he noted that "the decline of two empires, the Roman and the British, advance at the same pace". It was the last pleasantry. He had not lost his lightness of touch, but by then the war itself was

THE AMERICAN REVOLUTION

lost. The British successes in the South, the capture of
Savannah and Charleston, were illusive, and with the surrender of Cornwallis at Yorktown in the autumn of 1781 the
end came. Peace negotiations were opened in the following
year, and in 1783 in the Treaty of Paris the British recognized
American independence.

It might appear, from his silence in the Commons, that
Gibbon had been a witness of these great events but an imperfect judge of their importance. This impression is corrected
by his letters, in which he privately disclosed his apprehensions,
and by passages in *The Decline and Fall* which refute it entirely,
for one at least suggests a realization that America might one
day be both the refuge and the support of Europe.

As a writer, Gibbon was alive to the advantages of a new
continent for the English language, and he wrote in his
memoirs: "The conquests of our language and literature are
not confined to Europe alone, and a writer who succeeds in
London is speedily read on the banks of the Delaware . . ."
(*Autobiography*, p. 213.) In this he had perhaps been prompted
by Hume who, in the days when Gibbon was still composing
historical essays in French, wrote to him: "Let the French,
therefore, triumph in the present diffusion of their tongue. Our
solid and increasing establishments in America, where we need
less dread the inundation of Barbarians, promise a superior
stability and duration to the English language."

It may have been this too which inspired Gibbon's remarkable and prophetic passage at the end of his third
volume in which he held out a surer hope for the survival of
European civilization than had been the fate of the Roman
Empire:

If a savage conqueror should issue from the deserts of
Tartary, he must repeatedly vanquish the robust peasants

of Russia, the numerous armies of Germany, the gallant nobles of France, and the intrepid freemen of Britain, who, perhaps, might confederate for their common defence. Should the victorious barbarians carry slavery and desolation as far as the Atlantic Ocean, ten thousand vessels would transport beyond their pursuit the remains of civilised society; and Europe would revive and flourish in the American world, which is already filled with her colonies, and institutions. (iv, p. 187.)

To this Gibbon appended a note which gave further proof that he foresaw the greatness of America:

America now contains about six millions of European blood and descent; and their numbers, at least in the North, are continually increasing. Whatever may be the changes of their political situation, they must preserve the manners of Europe; and we may reflect with some pleasure, that the English language will probably be diffused over an immense and populous continent.

It might be too much to argue from this that Gibbon foresaw a time when the land mass of Russian Tartary and America would balance the world between them, but the emergence of Russia under Peter the Great had involved a revolution hardly less in its effects than the American one which he had viewed from the House of Commons. The importance of both seem to have been in his mind when he wrote, at the end of Chapter XLIII in *The Decline and Fall*, of the comet which had revisited the earth in seven equal revolutions of five hundred and seventy-five years, one of them in the reign of Justinian. Its last appearance had been investigated by Newton and Halley, and so Gibbon wrote:

THE AMERICAN REVOLUTION

At the *eighth* period, in the year two thousand three hundred and fifty-five, their calculations may perhaps be verified by the astronomers of some future capital in the Siberian or American wilderness. (iv, p. 463.)

XII

CITIZEN OF THE WORLD

I never was a very warm Patriot and I grow every day a
Citizen of the World.   (Letter of 21 March 1785.)

THE years of the American war, with attendance in the
House of Commons and in the fashionable houses of
London, had been a strain on Gibbon's finances, until they
were relieved by his income as a Lord of Trade. He received
some four thousand pounds for the first three volumes of *The
Decline and Fall*, but his father's estate had been left so
encumbered that the sum was rapidly absorbed. A further
strain on the estate was the income that had to be paid to his
step-mother, who was living in Bath. Yet the affection between
them was never disturbed by this. He was constantly writing
to reassure her, either on her income or his own health and
safety, for she had the double anxiety of the elderly, both
material and sentimental, on such matters. At the time of the
Gordon Riots in the summer of 1780 he wrote to her: "As
the old story of religion has raised most *formidable* tumults in
this town, and as they will of course seem much more formidable at the distance of a hundred miles, you may not be sorry
to hear that I am perfectly safe and well: my known attachment to the Protestant religion has most probably saved me."
In a letter three weeks later, recurring to this subject, he spoke
of a fanaticism "which I had supposed to be extinct, but which
actually subsists in Great Britain, perhaps beyond any other
country in Europe".

Though he had become English, he remained cosmopolitan in his sympathies. His native feelings were moderate. On a warm reference to Britain he observed in Chapter XIII of *The Decline and Fall*: "Notwithstanding our laudable partiality for our native country, it is difficult to conceive that, in the beginning of the fourth century, England deserved all these commendations." (i, p. 386*n.*)

This moderation was accompanied by a more urgent motive, one which affected so many in the golden age of the pound sterling, inducing him to leave his native country—the cheapness of living abroad. The loss of his position as a Lord of Trade in 1782 disorganized his finances anew. Some had criticized him for taking the office, and there was a story that a few days before accepting it he had been free in his criticism of the administration's American policy in conversation at Brook's. But quite apart from questions of policy, he had never nourished political ambition, and even the prospect of further office could hardly recompense him for the loss of valuable time, when he had already started on the Eastern Empire and was deep in the first of his last three volumes. "At the same time" he wrote in his memoirs "the tumult of London, and the attendance on parliament, were grown more irksome; and, without some additional income, I could not long or prudently maintain the style of expense to which I was accustomed." (*Autobiography*, p. 199.)

In these circumstances it was natural that his mind should turn to Lausanne, for there is one charm in the place where the most lively emotions of youth are experienced, another in the first foreign town to be visited, and Lausanne embodied both. At the age of forty-five Gibbon was in a mood to look back with nostalgia: "From my early acquaintance with Lausanne" he recalled "I had always cherished a secret wish that the school of my youth might become the retreat of my declining age."

How far the decision to move was the effect of this sentiment, how far the effect of economy, is not quite certain, but the sentiment was strong and genuine, for after his finances had recovered as a result of this judicious retreat, he was still reluctant to leave Lausanne, even when menaced by the approach of the French revolutionaries, for whom he had the strongest antipathy.

The decision was also influenced by the fact that his old friend Deyverdun, with whom he had discussed and even shared his first essays in historical writing, had inherited a pleasant property overlooking the Lake of Geneva. This encouraged Gibbon to propose that the two bachelors should set up house together, Deyverdun providing the home, and Gibbon undertaking its expenses: "His immediate answer was a warm and joyful acceptance."

Yet Gibbon admitted that he had to struggle against "the indolence of my temper, and the opinion of the world, which unanimously condemned this voluntary banishment". But he had abandoned the wearisome political round, and he was perhaps out of humour after the stress of the past ten years; it was in the year of his departure for Lausanne that he wrote a letter to the Unitarian Dr. Priestley which shows less than his usual urbanity, as he screwed his features into the distorted mask of a Christian apologist. Priestley, in his *History of the Corruptions of Christianity*, had issued a challenge to him, and his reply was that the public "will decide to whom the invidious name of *unbeliever* most justly belongs: to the historian, who, without interposing his own sentiments, has delivered a simple narrative of authentic facts, or to the disputant, who proudly rejects all natural proof of the immortality of the soul . . . and condemns the religion of every Christian nation as a fable". (Letter of 28 Jan. 1783.) In his memoirs he even suggested that Priestley's "trumpet of sedition may at length awaken the magistrates of a free country"—a sentiment most uncharacteristic of Gibbon. The letter's hypocrisy is hardly redeemed by its notable description of *The Decline and Fall*, "a simple narrative of authentic facts".

Of this simple narrative he had already finished the fourth volume before retiring to Lausanne, where he intended to complete the work in more peaceful surroundings and in easier circumstances.

The return to Lausanne justified his hopes. Already by December 1783, he was able to assert in a letter "that I have not repented a single moment of the step which I have taken and that I only regret the not having executed the same design two or five or even ten years ago".

He had taken his library with him, "a sacred deposit", and there above the Lake of Geneva, the one great water which, with its slopes of vines and its background of white mountains, has a Mediterranean calm and serenity, he was able to achieve his life's work without social strain or financial anxiety.

In the early autumn of 1785 a false report of his death was circulated in London, which provoked a lively reassurance to his friend Sheffield, revealing the easy humour of his life above the lake:

> ... the intelligence may be true. *Primo*, It must one day be true, and therefore may very probably be so at present. *Secundo*, We may always depend on the impartiality, accuracy, and veracity of an English newspaper. *Tertio*, which is indeed the strongest argument, we are credibly informed that for a long time past the said celebrated historian has not written to any of his friends in England ... he either is, or ought to be, dead.

> (Letter of 5 Sept. 1785.)

This letter is the more impressive in view of the fact that, when death really came nine years later, he approached it as lightly.

At last, two months after his fiftieth birthday, he came to the end of the Roman Empire, whose decline he had been tracing for the best part of twenty years:

> I have presumed to mark the moment of conception: I shall now commemorate the hour of my final deliverance. It was on the day, or rather night, of the 27th of June, 1787, between the hours of eleven and twelve, that I wrote the last lines of the last page, in a summer-house in my garden. After laying down my pen, I took several turns in a *berceau*, or covered walk of acacias, which commands a prospect of the country, the lake, and the mountains. The air was temperate, the sky was serene, the silver orb of the moon was reflected from the waters, and all nature was silent. I will not dissemble the first emotions of joy on recovery of my freedom, and, perhaps, the establishment of my fame. But my pride was soon humbled, and a sober melancholy was spread over my mind, by the idea that I had taken an everlasting leave of an old and agreeable companion . . .
>
> (*Autobiography*, p. 205.)

In the same year he returned to England to guide his work through the press: "After a quiet residence of four years, during which I had never moved ten miles from Lausanne, it was not without reluctance that I undertook, in a journey of two hundred leagues, to cross the mountains and the sea." (*Autobiography*, p. 206.)

His home in England was "Lord Sheffield's house and library", both at Sheffield Place in Sussex and in London at Downing Street. "In the larger circle of the metropolis I observed the country and the inhabitants with the knowledge, and without the prejudices, of an Englishman." Those prejudices had never taken proper root in him, for he was never long enough at school to have them instilled in him by friends or masters, while Oxford had alienated him in more ways than one, and the five years at Lausanne, in which he had grown to manhood, had made him an alien in fact, more fluent in French than in his native tongue. He claimed that his service with the militia had turned him into an Englishman, but he never relished the company of his fellow officers and country squires, and when he began his Grand Tour he found more doors open to him in Paris than in London, where the friends he later made were themselves more cosmopolitan—the nucleus of them being, strangely enough, those whose acquaintance he had made abroad. Even they had not been sufficient to keep him in England, and now that he was in London he had no intention of settling, but returned to Lausanne in the following year, 1788, once he had seen his last three volumes through the press. Even while in London one of his occupations was showing the town to a young friend from Switzerland, Wilhelme de Severy, whose family had become as close to him there as the Sheffields were in England—with both families he had the easy standing commonly associated with indulgent bachelor uncles, welcome with the women and children.

In London he was a citizen of the world, but also a citizen of the Roman Empire, which was already and inseparably linked with his name. On more than one occasion on this visit, he had pleasant reminders of his fame.

He attended the trial of Warren Hastings, for whose "persecution" he had some sympathy, perhaps because it recalled what his grandfather, another victim of party battles, had endured in the time of the South Sea Bubble. But Sheridan's tremendous speech could not fail to stir him, especially in its reference that "nothing equal in criminality was to be traced, either in ancient or modern history, in the correct periods of Tacitus or the luminous page of Gibbon". It was maliciously rumoured that this last phrase had been altered, in his hearing, to "the voluminous pages of Gibbon", as the six great volumes acquired among the frivolous an aspect of heaviness—most unjustly, for it is doubtful whether any other work of such bulk has so much literary grace and lightness.

Far heavier were the poetic tributes, with which minor poets raise their voices but not their gifts to salute greatness, that greeted the work, among them Hayley's "Occasional Stanzas", in which England was ordered to exult:

> Science for thee a Newton raised;
> For thy renown a Shakespeare blazed,
>   Lord of the drama's sphere!
> In different fields to equal praise
> See History now thy Gibbon raise
>   To shine without a peer!

Yet such tributes could only gratify the vanity, if not the taste, of the historian. It was of more moment that his work was appearing in French, Italian, and German translations, more proper tributes to the cosmopolitan spirit of the author, who admitted that in the last three volumes "the constant habit of speaking one language and writing another may have infused some mixture of Gallic idioms". (*Autobiography*, p. 204.)

But there were other, and more important points, in which they differed from the first three.

XIII

BYZANTIUM

The division of the Roman world between the sons of Theodosius, marks the final establishment of the Empire of the East, which, from the reign of Arcadius to the taking of Constantinople by the Turks, subsisted one thousand and fifty-eight years, in a state of premature and perpetual decay.

(*The Decline and Fall*, ch. xxxii (vol. iii, p. 378).)

THIS foretaste to Gibbon's treatment of the Eastern Empire had already appeared in his third volume, revealing his antipathy to the Byzantine tradition. This antipathy radically altered the character of his work in the last three volumes of *The Decline and Fall*, for it meant that he no longer stood at the centre of his theme, no longer wrote history as a novel with Rome as the hero of it. Throughout the first three volumes, Rome, even when the decline became more abrupt, had remained at least a noble ghost, like that of Hamlet's father, to brood significantly over the whole drama; but without that august figure the last three volumes came nearer to resembling Hamlet without the Prince of Denmark.

It is true that Rome reappears in the course of them, to make a memorable final appearance in the last pages, but that distorts more than it improves the perspective, for Gibbon, as if jealous of Byzantium's claim to be the Second Rome, constantly preferred the West before the East, becoming, oddly enough, the spokesman of that western religious tradition which, based on the schism between the Roman and the Greek Churches, has developed today into the view of the West as the champion of liberal ideas against the Caesarism of the East. As in the last century Russians had claimed that Moscow, as the heir of Byzantium, was the Third Rome, this view has also been involved in wider political and cultural controversies.

For Gibbon there was only one Rome, and it is perhaps in his devotion to Rome that the explanation of his antipathy to Byzantium is to be found. In exposing the constant decline in the West, as in Chapter XXXIX, early in the fourth volume, when he wrote of Theodoric that "a rude mark was contrived to represent the signature of the illiterate King of Italy" (iv, p. 183), he was less prepared to concede that culture had taken refuge in Byzantium, which preserved the Roman tradition more actively than Rome until the Renaissance, to which she also made an important contribution.

Gibbon was, too, less learned in Greek than in Latin, and he had little sympathy with the Greek philosophic temper, even before it had insinuated itself into abstruse theological speculations which aroused his sharpest irony. After he had finished *The Decline and Fall*, he says in his memoirs (*Autobiography*, p. 214): "I involved myself in the philosophic maze of the writings of Plato, of which the dramatic is, perhaps, more interesting than the argumentative part"—a singular judgment, offensive to philosophers, in which Macaulay was later to concur.

But it was his Roman sympathy, more than his intellectual distaste for the Greek mind, which led him to speak of the Eastern Empire as being for over a thousand years "in a state of premature and perpetual decay", a paradox which refutes itself when set against the fact that this empire was constantly fighting for its own and civilization's existence until the last day in 1453 when the Turks breached the walls of its capital and the last emperor, Constantine Palaeologus, died fighting.

BYZANTIUM

Gibbon was the heir of long prejudices against the Byzantine Empire which remained lively in the eighteenth century: Horace Walpole, who had said that "Gibbon never tires me", found it "a disgusting subject". These prejudices survived into the nineteenth century when Lecky, in his *History of European Morals*, wrote of that empire that "the universal verdict of history is that it constitutes the most base and despicable form that civilisation ever assumed".

Yet George Finlay, in his studies, had already vindicated the Byzantine achievement when Lecky wrote, enabling Cotter Morison to assert: "Next in time, but hardly second in value to the services of the Greeks at Marathon and Salamis, must be reckoned the services of the Byzantine emperors in repelling the barbarians."

Yet the prejudice against Byzantium died hard. The private lives of the emperors were abhorred by some who had more indulgence for those of western monarchs. Lecky spoke of their "perpetual fratricide", causing Oman to protest that between the years 340 and 1453 not a single emperor had been murdered by a brother, only one dethroned by a brother. Some of the charges were based on Greek writers themselves—unjustly, because it was the strength of their moral and religious feelings which they exhibited more faithfully than the corruption of the Byzantine court; and Oman commented that "Every moralist, from Jeremiah to Juvenal, and from Juvenal to Ruskin, has believed his own generation to be the most obnoxious and the most contemptible in the world's history."

In recent years the Byzantine Empire has received more justice, with the result that Gibbon's last three volumes are today perhaps treated with more reserve than his earlier chapters on Christianity, for these were true enough in the perspective of his deist philosophy and Roman loyalty, but his account of the Byzantine Empire shows faults in historical perspective, equally visible to those who accept or those who reject the Christian tradition. These faults were the more serious because Gibbon was the one great British historian to produce a coherent narrative of the vital thousand years between the end of the Western Empire and the Renaissance, which were responsible for "the making of Europe", and in his book of that name Mr. Christopher Dawson regrets that "even the greatest of our historians of the Eastern Empire— Edward Gibbon—shows a complete lack of sympathy for its culture; to him it is simply an appendix to Roman history".

Gibbon was too much of a senatorial Roman to welcome either the Christian empire of Constantine or his founding of Constantinople. Between that time in the first half of the fourth century and the Persian wars of Heraclius in the first half of the seventh century, which were contemporary with the rise of Mahomet, the Eastern Empire was progressively deromanized—already Justinian, born towards the end of the fifth century, was the last emperor to be Latin-speaking by birth. These changes had their part in alienating Gibbon's sympathies. He might have admired Justinian as one of the last great imperial figures and the codifier of Roman law, but he had no sympathy with the emperor's theological interests and as little with his traditional character in Byzantine art.

It is the revival of interest in that art, later stimulated by El Greco and his relation to Cubism, that has led to a new estimate of Byzantine culture as a whole. Writing as recently as 1937, Mr. D. M. Low could still claim that "even the modern interest in Byzantine art is lukewarm". It has since increased, but in the eighteenth century, with its classical standards, that art was still hidden. When Gibbon visited Venice in 1765, he wrote of "stinking ditches dignified with the pompous denomination of canals . . . and a large square decorated with the worst architecture I ever yet saw". (Letter of 22 April 1765.)

With this view of its architecture, he also underestimated the importance of Venice and of the Exarchate of Ravenna in their constant influence on the West. He had as little sympathy for the art as for the religion of Byzantium, and it is significant that the most recent protagonist of Byzantine civilization, Mr. Steven Runciman, should maintain that "its Church remained the most civilised religious organization that the world has so far known". The same writer emphasizes the otherworldly character of that civilization—precisely the side that was veiled from Gibbon—to conclude his study with the noble words: "What was the Emperor, the Peer of the Apostles, what even was Constantinople itself, the great City dear to God and to his Mother, compared to Christ Pantocrator and the glorious Courts of Heaven?"

If Mr. Runciman, as a Byzantine scholar, should be suspected of too warm a sympathy for his subject, Mr. Dawson, whom none would accuse of hostility to the Western tradition, is no less strong in asserting that the Byzantine Empire, up to 1000, "remained by far the greatest European power and the chief surviving representative of higher culture in the West. But while it is difficult to exaggerate the importance of the Byzantine influences on mediaeval culture, it is no less difficult to exaggerate the strength of the oriental influences on Byzantine culture itself".

These oriental influences affected the Eastern Empire no less profoundly than the barbarian invasions changed the West, for in both there was a double process of resistance and absorption. From the time of Heraclius in the seventh century to the fall of the capital in the fifteenth century, the Eastern Empire was constantly beset by the followers of Mahomet, yet maintained by a defence that was only irretrievably weakened after the battle of Manzikert in 1071, which lost the rich corn-lands and hardy peasants of Asia Minor.

But Gibbon, for whom the "sublime" creed of Mahomet was a contrast to the "corruptions" of Christianity, was less impressed by the importance of this struggle than he had been by the defence of the Western Empire against the barbarians. When Charles Martel repels the Saracens at the battle of Tours in 732, Gibbon can still indulge one of his most charming fancies on a different outcome of the fighting:

> Perhaps the interpretation of the Koran would now be taught in the schools of Oxford, and her pulpits might demonstrate to a circumcised people the sanctity and truth of the revelation of Mahomet.

So he wrote in Chapter LII of *The Decline and Fall* (vi, p. 16), but he was less inspired by the Byzantine emperors' defence of their eastern provinces.

In underestimating both the military and cultural importance of the Byzantine Empire, even for western Europe, he may also have been influenced by his real partiality for the creed of Mahomet. Certainly some of his finest passages occur in these chapters in which he treats of the Arabs, for whose lands he reveals that sympathy which has inspired so many English writers.

His description of Arabia in Chapter L is one of his best essays in the geography which so enlivens his history:

> The entire surface of the peninsula exceeds in a fourfold proportion that of Germany or France; but the far greater part has been justly stigmatised with the epithets of the *stony* and the *sandy*. Even the wilds of Tartary are decked, by the hand of nature, with lofty trees and luxuriant herbage; and the lonesome traveller derives a sort of comfort and society from the presence of vegetable life. But in the

dreary waste of Arabia, a boundless level of sand is inter-
sected by sharp and naked mountains; and the face of the
desert, without shade or shelter, is scorched by the direct
and intense rays of a tropical sun. Instead of refreshing
breezes, the winds, particularly from the south-west, diffuse
a noxious and even deadly vapour; the hillocks of sand
which they alternately raise and scatter, are compared to the
billows of the ocean, and whole caravans, whole armies,
have been lost and buried in the whirlwind. The common
benefits of water are an object of desire and contest; and such
is the scarcity of wood, that some art is required to preserve
and propagate the element of fire. Arabia is destitute of
navigable rivers, which fertilise the soil, and convey its
produce to the adjacent regions: the torrents that fall from
the hills are imbibed by the thirsty earth: the rare and hardy
plants, the tamarind or the acacia, that strike their roots into
the clefts of the rocks, are nourished by the dews of the
night: a scanty supply of rain is collected in cisterns and
aqueducts: the wells and springs are the secret treasure of
the desert: and the pilgrim of Mecca, after many a dry and
sultry march, is disgusted by the taste of the waters, which
have rolled over a bed of sulphur or salt. Such is the general
and genuine picture of the climate of Arabia.

(v, pp. 333–4.)

A page or two later, he gives a description of the camel
hardly less classical:

In the sands of Africa and Arabia, the *camel* is a sacred
and precious gift. That strong and patient beast of burden
can perform, without eating or drinking, a journey of
several days; and a reservoir of fresh water is preserved in a
large bag, a fifth stomach of the animal, whose body is

imprinted with the marks of servitude: the larger breed is capable of transporting a weight of a thousand pounds: and the dromedary, of a lighter and more active frame, outstrips the fleetest courser in the race. Alive or dead, almost every part of the camel is serviceable to man: her milk is plentiful and nutritious: the young and tender flesh has the taste of veal: a valuable salt is extracted from the urine: the dung supplies the deficiency of fuel; and the long hair, which falls each year and is renewed, is coarsely manufactured into the garments, the furniture, and the tents of the Bedouins.

(v, p. 337.)

For the Arabs, Gibbon had something more than the philosophical sympathy of a deist, because their strength and flexibility in the greatest days of their rule had in it the Roman virtue which he most admired. Yet the Byzantine Empire, despite its Greek theological subtleties, which provoked his irony or his distaste, had at least its naval and commercial greatness and that smooth diplomacy which has so often eased the progress of empire; and it preserved contact even with the extreme West, as is shown by the fact that Englishmen with their battle-axes, escaping from their country after the Norman invasion, enrolled in the Varangian guard of the Byzantine Empire, to use those axes against the Normans, who attacked its domains no less fiercely than the island of Britain. Gibbon himself, in Chapter LV, pays tribute to this "numerous band" who "preserved, till the last age of the empire, the inheritance of spotless loyalty, and the use of the Danish or English tongue".

For such points of historical interest, he had a brilliant eye, no less remarkable than his compression of them into an absorbing narrative. But while he could create an almost perfect geographical summary, such as his description of Arabia quoted above, or his conspectus of Constantinople or of

Rome, he was less perfect in historical summary and comparison, partly owing to the timeless equality of his temperament and the smooth texture of his narration. Even his first three volumes have been criticized on the grounds that, while he notes such facts as depopulation, agricultural decay, and increasing taxation, he fails to summarize them and assess their part in the decline of the Empire. But the last three volumes, as they covered a far wider span of history—over a thousand years—and embraced a greater number of peoples and places, from Tartary to the ultimate Thule of Britain, had to rely far more on the power to summarize. As summaries, these chapters are masterpieces of compressed narrative, but though each chapter is masterly in itself, there is a lack of unity in the whole, because there is no dominant theme, such as Rome herself supplied in the earlier volumes.

Gibbon could not allow that Byzantium, the Second Rome, exercised the same fertile and maternal influence on the peoples of eastern Europe as Rome herself on those of the West. Yet the greatness of the Byzantine Empire was not only in its influence on the West, but in its more lasting effect on the Bulgarian and the Serbian empires, and on the Russians until they were overwhelmed by the Mongol invasions of the thirteenth century.

Here it is interesting to contrast Gibbon's view of the Eastern Empire with that of a recent writer drawing on Russian sources. Mr. Jack Lindsay, in his *Byzantium into Europe*, emphasizes just this aspect of the Byzantine achievement. Although writing from a Communist point of view, he is more sympathetic than Gibbon to Christianity, for he sees this as a revolutionary movement, with Athanasius and early monasticism as the rise of a popular party, while the Nestorians and the Monophysites figure as a resistance to imperial authority. Gibbon's limitations, for Mr. Lindsay, result from the tension between "the liberal and the conservative elements" in him, while "the historical consciousness developed out of the inner conflict in his society" makes him aware of "a menace, a deep crisis shaking his world".

It is difficult to reconcile this with Gibbon's serenity and urbanity, while the contrast between the liberal and conservative elements in him is more apparent than real, for his politics were wholly conservative; his liberalism was intellectual only, that of a man without any religion or philosophy beyond a vague deism. But Mr. Lindsay provides a valuable commentary on Gibbon precisely because he has a coherent philosophy of his own, which Gibbon lacked. So he can see the larger significance of the Byzantine Empire, because he can look beyond the immediate historical scene. It is both Gibbon's greatness and his weakness as a historian that he rarely rises above history. His one great belief, in Rome and the practical values of civilization, was attenuated in the uncertain conflicts of the Dark Ages, which have a meaning for those who see in them the survival of the Christian faith. Gibbon was so beguiled by Rome and the return to her standards at the Renaissance that he saw this not as the culmination of a thousand years' history, but as a reaction against it. In his view the Byzantine Empire contributed so little to the civilization of his own day that he could dismiss it, as in Chapter XLVIII, as "a dead uniformity of abject vices, which are neither softened by the weakness of humanity, nor animated by the vigour of memorable crimes". (v, p. 181.) This attitude to the Eastern Empire inevitably gave a western tinge to his whole work, which is the real grounds of the protest by Mr. Lindsay, who is seeking to redress the balance in favour of the East, and who is equally critical of Professor Toynbee for making as pointed a contrast between the traditions of western and eastern Europe.

BYZANTIUM

Mr. Geoffrey Barraclough, in the essays assembled in *History in a Changing World*, is no less on his guard against this erection of a spiritual barrier between West and East, and declares that the experience of the last war demands a broadening of the whole scope of history in the West, which has so long neglected the importance of eastern Europe.

Gibbon at least was the first to remedy that neglect, and his superb literary gifts have won him readers who would be repelled by works designed more narrowly to instruct than to please. If he lacked sympathy with Christianity and with the Byzantine Empire, he at least had the most vivid and the most generous sympathy with history itself, with great events, with great men, with great cities.

Sometimes he could even rise above his own limitations and record an event with the emotion of a contemporary, as when he wrote in Chapter LVII of the origin of the Crusades that "a nerve was touched of exquisite feeling; and the sensation vibrated to the heart of Europe" (v, p. 268), though two chapters later he was referring with his more usual irony to "the desperate adventure of possessing or recovering a tombstone two thousand miles from their country". (vi, p. 345.)

In the religious sphere, he is sometimes defective, even as a historian, in his omissions. The religious figures who had so great an influence in the centuries he was describing receive his attention if they arouse his political sense or his no less acute sense of the ridiculous, but others, some of them crucial, are omitted—among them St. Boniface, a man, Mr. Dawson maintains, who had "a deeper influence on the history of Europe than any Englishman who has ever lived". Certainly Gibbon was not dealing directly with the history of the Germans, but in his summary in Chapter XLIX he might have found space for their conversion.

Mr. Michael Joyce brings out this point well when he says

that while we read of Gibbon's amusement in Chapter XXXVII that "the name and genius of Simeon Stylites have been immortalised by the singular invention of an aerial penance" (iv, p. 79), there is less revealed on the other side, and "we hear nothing" says Mr. Joyce "of the more sublime extravagance with which St. Francis of Assisi kissed the leper."

Yet St. Francis would not have been out of place as a footnote to the Crusades, though far more significant in a deeper estimate of medieval history; and that this was beyond Gibbon's scope shows how selective his summaries of those centuries were.

These omissions were the more important because Gibbon's last three volumes, though not the better part of his work, had the greater influence because they were the first and the best treatment in English of a neglected period of European history. He performed the magnificent service to his generation, and to succeeding generations, of restoring unity both in time and place, enabling English readers to see both the ages which had formed them and the continent to which they belonged. He was read with interest and with profit, and it was nearly a century before his omissions were rectified, even among scholars, longer still before a wider view could reach a more general public.

Perhaps, too, the circulation of these three volumes was aided by some of their anecdotes, of a sort more usually associated with popular lives of royal mistresses. "I never could understand" wrote Gibbon in his memoirs "the clamour that has been raised against the indecency of my three last volumes." He claimed that he had used the same freedom in earlier chapters, and that "my English text is chaste, and all licentious passages are left in the obscurity of a learned language". (*Autobiography*, pp. 211–12.)

It is at least true that he used a freedom more customary in

French than in English. But it was a French critic, Sainte-Beuve, who spoke of his "cold and erudite obscenity", though certainly Sainte-Beuve, besides being the most eminent of critics, was also the historian of the Jansenists. His mention of "erudite" in this connection helps to identify Gibbon, for he had the sort of taste, not altogether uncommon among bachelors of arts, which relishes shocking incidents in historical corners, not only in the ordinary masculine way, but with an appreciation of the extra research involved in uncovering them, so that it might be described as an occupational disease among scholars, who naturally cherish the fruits of their labours. Certainly Gibbon cherished his.

But this was not an isolated trait in his character. He had been at some pains to become a man of the world and, having succeeded, he easily adopted that mocking attitude to women and religion proper to the character, never more fashionable than in the eighteenth century. This is not to imply that his feelings towards women and religion were false. They were genuine enough, but the expression of them was influenced by a worldly prejudice. Nor is it an accident that he so wholly shared his age's suspicion of "enthusiasm", for it is precisely the power, common to both religion and women, of raising men to such extravagances of feeling, that causes men of the world to arm themselves against them with aloofness or with irony. Such detachment is intensified when it is combined with an aristocratic cast of mind—and the outbreak of the French Revolution revealed how essentially aristocratic was Gibbon's whole outlook.

XIV

THE FRENCH REVOLUTION

> . . . my own contempt for the wild and mischievous system
> of Democracy.   (Letter of 24 June 1793.)

AFTER his return from London, where he had published
the last volumes of *The Decline and Fall* and secured his
fame, to Lausanne in July 1788, Gibbon had a fair prospect of
carefree years before him. He was only a year over fifty and
calculated that he might expect to enjoy another fifteen, in
which, as he wrote to Sheffield, he could "range without control over the wide expanse of my library; converse as my
fancy prompts me, with poets and historians, philosophers and
orators, of every age and language; and often indulge my
meditations in the invention and arrangement of mighty
works, which I shall probably never find time or application to
execute". (Letter of 4 Oct. 1788.) Nor was he wanting in
companions of flesh and blood—in the same year he had a visit
from Fox, who "gave me, in a few words, such a character of
Pitt, as one great man should give of another his rival: much
of books, from my own, on which he flattered me very
pleasantly, to Homer and the *Arabian Nights*". At that time,
this return to the two books which he had so enjoyed with his
aunt in childhood had in it no omen of a completed circle, yet
in fact he had only another five and a half years to live.

Already in the following year, 1789, two events, one private,
the other immensely public, broke into the calm lake of his
life. The first was the death of Deyverdun, the friend of his

first years in Lausanne, the companion of his uncertain years in England before he had identified himself with *The Decline and Fall*, and finally the partner of his home. Gibbon, aided by his will, was able to come to terms with the heir for life-possession of the property, but there was no consolation for the personal loss. "I must reluctantly observe" he wrote at the end of his *Autobiography* (p. 221) "that two causes, the abbreviation of time, and the failure of hope, will always tinge with a browner shade the evening of life." Yet at Lausanne Gibbon had found "as much happiness as is compatible with human nature", and still believed that "no other place is so well adapted to my taste and habits of studious and social life". (Letter of 9 Sept. 1789.)

The other event which broke the calm surface and upset Lausanne itself with an influx of French refugees was the revolution in France. Gibbon's first comment on this has an oddly modern sound: "What a scene is France! While the Assembly is voting abstract propositions, Paris is an independent republic; the provinces have neither authority nor freedom, and poor Necker declares that credit is no more, and that the people refuse to pay taxes." Another echo, revealing the continuity of the English ruling class, comes a line or two later in the same letter to Sheffield: "If Eden goes to Paris, you may have some curious information."

Gibbon's reaction to the events in France was at first judicious and detached:

What would you have me say of the affairs of France? We are too near, and too remote, to form an accurate judgement of that wonderful scene. The abuses of the court and government called aloud for reformation; and it has happened, as it will always happen, that an innocent well-disposed Prince has paid the forfeit of the sins of his predecessors; of the ambition of Lewis the Fourteenth, of the profusion of Lewis the Fifteenth. The French nation had a glorious opportunity, but they have abused and may lose their advantages. If they had been content with a liberal translation of our system, if they had respected the prerogatives of the crown, and the privileges of the nobles, they might have raised a solid fabric on the only true foundation, the natural aristocracy of a great country.

(Letter of 15 Dec. 1789.)

That had long been Gibbon's conviction. In Chapter LX of *The Decline and Fall* he had praised in Venice "the wise and jealous aristocracy, which has reduced the doge to a pageant, and the people to a cipher" (vi, p. 398)—not very different from the English aristocracy of the eighteenth century, whose government Gibbon had approved in the House of Commons.

But he was already looking for a Napoleon to restore order in France: "As yet, there is no symptom of a great man, a Richelieu or a Cromwell, arising either to restore the monarchy, or to lead the commonwealth."

Yet, despite "the Gallic frenzy, the wild theories of equal and boundless freedom", his normal life was not disturbed, and his letters to Sheffield intersperse French news with requests to his wine merchant: "Pray take serious strenuous measures for sending me a pipe of excellent Madeira in cask, with some dozens of Malmsey Madeira." In another letter he added: "Good Madeira is now become essential to my health and reputation. May your hogshead prove as good as the last; may it not be intercepted by the rebels or the Austrians."

In the spring of 1790 he had an attack of gout, perhaps not unconnected with his addiction to Madeira—"such a fit of the gout as I had never known, though I must be thankful that its dire effects have been confined to the feet and knees, without ascending to the more noble parts." (Letter of 15 May 1790.)

In the same year he renewed contact with the Neckers, who had returned to Switzerland, uprooted by the storm in Paris. Necker himself was bowed by the blow, but Suzanne showed more composure in the presence of her old lover, to whom she afterwards wrote: "You have always been dear to me, but the friendship you have shown to M. Necker adds to that which you inspire me with on so many grounds, and I love you at present with a double affection."

Gibbon and Suzanne could admire each other more reasonably, if more dispassionately, than in their early days, for both had achieved the success which the consciousness of their own qualities had led them to expect of life. Neither could arouse the envy of the other, for the wife of the great financial minister was a match for the great historian. Perhaps she had the greater, the feminine, loyalty to her youth and her lover—and also the satisfaction of finding him still single.

Possibly too he had moments of regret, for it was after seeing her again that he wrote to Sheffield, declaring that he could not contemplate marriage to any of those who pleased him most: "Yet I feel and shall continue to feel, that domestic solitude, however it may be alleviated by the world, by study, and even by friendship, is a comfortless state, which will grow more painful as I descend in the vale of years."

At the same time, he was feeling the need of a nurse, having more pain than he had ever experienced with the gout. It was during this illness that Suzanne wrote to him: "Come to us when you are restored to health and to yourself; that moment should always belong to your first and your last friend, and I do not know which of those titles is the sweetest and dearest to my heart."

He recovered and was soon more anxious about public affairs: "Poor France! the state is dissolved, the nation is mad!" But in the spring of 1791 he was able to raise the spirits of Lausanne by giving a ball in which he was aided by the Severys, who remained his closest friends there, and in the summer he had a visit from the Sheffields, who were his closest friends and most frequent correspondents in England.

Visiting him at his home in Lausanne, Lord Sheffield noted that "from early youth Mr. Gibbon had contracted a partiality for foreign taste and foreign habits of life, which made him less a stranger abroad than he was, in some respects, in his native country". He also noticed the trend of his opinions on French affairs which had caused him to become "a warm and zealous advocate for every sort of old establishment, which he marked in various ways, sometimes rather ludicrously". The ludicrous occasion was when Gibbon seemed seriously to argue in favour of the Inquisition at Lisbon, so attached had the march of time made him to venerable institutions.

The Sheffields' visit gave pleasure on both sides, and Gibbon marked its happy progress in a letter written on their return to England:

> I could never understand how two persons of such superior merit, as Miss Holroyd and Miss Lausanne, could have so little relish for one another, as they appeared to have in the beginning; and it was with great pleasure that I observed the degrees of their growing intimacy, and the mutual regret of their separation.
>
> (Letter of 9 Nov. 1791.)

By the spring of 1792 he was apprehensive that the contagion of revolution might spread to England and warned

Sheffield that "if you do not resist the spirit of innovation in the first attempt, if you admit the smallest and most specious change in our parliamentary system, you are lost".

By August he was convinced that "this total subversion of all rank, order, and government could be productive only of a popular monster, which after devouring everything else, must finally devour itself", an opinion later to be endorsed by one of the revolutionaries who said, when so many of its leaders had gone to the guillotine, that the revolution, like Saturn, had devoured its own children.

Gibbon had formed a project for returning the Sheffields' visit by going to them in England, but he wrote that "so unwieldy and inactive a being" was reluctant to move, especially as the French troubles had increased the difficulties of travel. In a reference to the Sheffields' kindness to French refugees, he wrote in the autumn of 1792: "Should I even be forced to take refuge in England (a violent measure so late in the year), you would perhaps receive me as kindly as you do the French priests—a noble act of hospitality."

In that same autumn his comments on French affairs were more vigorous: ". . . the last revolution of Paris appears to have convinced almost everybody of the fatal consequences of democratical principles, which lead by a path of flowers into the abyss of hell." In another letter he returned more strongly to the same image, "the blackest demon in hell, the demon of democracy". (Letters of 23 Aug. and 8 Nov. 1792.)

Some have suggested, in view of this language, that Gibbon was thrown off his balance by the French Revolution and renounced some of his own principles. So tremendous an event, breaking so late and so closely into his life, might have been expected to have such an effect, but in fact there are similar references to democracy in the early chapters of *The*

Decline and Fall, long before the French, and even before the American, revolution.

In a reference to the administration of Augustus in Chapter III he wrote: "The assemblies of the people were for ever abolished, and the emperors were delivered from a dangerous multitude, who, without restoring liberty, might have disturbed, and perhaps endangered, the established government." (i, pp. 73–4.) In the beginning of the same chapter, in a general disquisition on government, he admitted the advantage of a "stubborn commons" as a guard against despotism, but before these he placed "a martial nobility". His anti-clerical opinions might be adduced as evidence of democratic sympathies, for he added in the same passage that "the banner of the church has very seldom been seen on the side of the people" (i, p. 65), a remark which one of his editors, Oliphant Smeaton, dismisses with a generalization hardly less exact as "wholly incorrect"; and there is far more truth in the assertion of his greatest biographer, Mr. D. M. Low, that "his banners were not likely to be found on the side of the people".

This is borne out by another remark at the beginning of Chapter VII in *The Decline and Fall* that "we shall cheerfully acquiesce in any expedient which deprives the multitude of the dangerous, and indeed the ideal, power of giving themselves a master". (i, p. 181.)

In Gibbon's letters written during the progress of the revolution, these opinions are naturally produced in a more lively form, exaggerated both by the easier medium and the pressure of events, but they are essentially the same. With him, as with the majority of men, there is little evidence of change either in his political or in his religious opinions after the age of thirty, when he had returned from his Grand Tour and conceived the plan of *The Decline and Fall*.

He became, in the winter of 1792, more apprehensive of the revolution as he saw the success of the French arms, but that was a natural and general fear, common to men of all parties. He noted that the officers, though "scarcely a gentleman among them", kept "a rough kind of discipline" over their men. There was cause enough for alarm, as "they conquer Savoy, pillage Germany, threaten Spain: the Low Countries are ere now invaded; Rome and Italy tremble; they scour the Mediterranean, and talk of sending a squadron into the South Sea". (Letter of 10 Nov. 1792.)

Yet he maintained his serenity, as was shown in a postscript to this letter which declared:

> The revolution of France, and my triple dispatch by the same post to Sheffield Place, are, in my opinion, the two most singular events in the eighteenth century.

Even his fears about democracy's spreading to England were lightly expressed: " ... if you begin to improve the constitution you may be driven step by step from the disfranchisement of old Sarum to the King in Newgate, the Lords voted useless, the Bishops abolished, and a House of Commons without articles (*sans culottes*)." Even in regretting of Fox that "his inmost soul was deeply tinged with democracy", he had later to add: "Let him do what he will, I must love the dog." (Letters of 25 Nov. 1792; 1 Jan. and 6 Jan. 1793.)

At the beginning of 1793, considering again a visit to England, he confessed to "a sort of curiosity to spend some days at Paris, to assist at the debates of the Pandemonium, to seek an introduction to the principal devils, and to contemplate a new form of public and private life, which never existed before, and which I devoutly hope will not long continue to exist".

He not only preserved this lightness of tone, but also the judgment of the historian who foresaw the devastation of the revolutionary wars:

> The French are strong in numbers, activity, and enthusiasm; they are rich in rapine; and, although their strength may be only that of a frenzy fever, they may do infinite mischief to their neighbours before they can be reduced to a strait-waistcoat. (Letter of 18 Feb. 1793.)

When the serenity of his correspondence to Sheffield was broken, it was not by any public event, but by the news of Lady Sheffield's death. At once, in spite of the difficulties and dangers of the journey, which had not diminished since he last abandoned the project, and in spite of the indolence of his body which was not less but more "unwieldy" than before, he resolved to cross the mountains and the sea to console his old friend: "The only consolation in these melancholy trials to which human life is exposed, the only one at least in which I have any confidence, is the presence of a real friend; and of that, as far as it depends on myself, you shall not be destitute."

It was a noble decision, one that does much to redeem Gibbon from the charge of coldness sometimes brought against him. It was taken, moreover, within eight months of his own death.

His kindness and generosity were also evident in his letters of consolation to Sheffield, even at the expense of his own opinions: "But she is now at rest; and if there be a future life, her mild virtues have surely entitled her to the reward of pure and perfect felicity." And again: "If there be any invisible guardians, may they watch over you and yours!" There is something very moving in this double witness to the generosity and to the truth of his own heart, for in qualifying the phrases as he did, he only increased their sincerity.

So in May 1793, he quitted Lausanne and, passing through Germany, sometimes in sound of the French guns, reached Brussels and Ostend, where he embarked for England, separated for ever from the Lausanne in which he had suffered the deepest emotions and known the greatest tranquillity of his life.

XV

THE NOBLEST ROMAN

This was the noblest Roman of them all;
All the conspirators save only he
Did that they did in envy of great Caesar;
He only, in a general honest thought
And common good to all, made one of them.
(Shakespeare, *Julius Caesar*, V, v.)

He observed to me that it was a very bad sign *with him* when he could not eat his breakfast, which he had done at all times very heartily; and this seems to have been the strongest expression of apprehension that he was ever observed to utter.
(Lord Sheffield, note in Gibbon's *Autobiography*, p. 332.)

ON his return to England in the summer of 1793 at the age of fifty-six, after a journey which might have tried the patience and the health of a younger man, Gibbon went at once to Sheffield's house in Downing Street and then to Sheffield Place in Sussex for the rest of the summer. He made use of the summer and the countryside in his usual manner, by staying indoors. In the autumn, he went to Bath to visit his stepmother, who "has spirits, appetite, legs, and eyes, and talks of living to ninety".

In November, back in London, he admitted to being "fatigued, and rather unwell". As, according to Sheffield, he was "inclined to represent his health as better than it really was", there was cause for anxiety, especially when a day later he confessed: "I am still awkward, though without any suspicions of gout, and have some idea of having recourse to medical advice." But it was not until 11th November, four days after the first admission, that he revealed to Sheffield the truth of a condition which had been with him for many years:

> I must at length withdraw the veil before my state of health, though the naked truth may alarm you more than a fit of the gout. Have you never observed, through my *inexpressibles*, a large prominency which, as it was not at all painful, and very little troublesome, I had strangely neglected for many years? But since my departure from Sheffield Place it has increased (most stupendously), is increasing, and ought to be diminished.
>
> (Letter of 11 Nov. 1793.)

Such was the genial pleasantry with which he announced the disability which was to cause his death. The surgeons declared that it was "a hydrocele (a collection of water), which must be let out by the operation of tapping; but, from its magnitude and long neglect, they think it a most extraordinary case", as indeed it was, for the protuberance had long been visible to the most casual observer. Six years before, Sheffield had been alarmed and had discreetly spoken to Gibbon's valet, who told him that his master much disliked any allusion to the subject. Even so, Sheffield had privately consulted "some medical persons" who supposed that it was a rupture and that precautions had been taken. There the matter had rested.

Gibbon's neglect of the condition appeared strange to the surgeons, but it was not out of character, for he was by nature serene and optimistic, having also that mixture of indolence, vanity, and confidence which commonly leads middle-aged men to rest assured of their health. Further, he had all his life the stoicism which he exhibited so signally in this last illness. Perhaps, too, he had a certain prudery, owing to the nature of the complaint, for he concluded the letter in which he broke the news to Sheffield by saying: "Varnish the business for the ladies; yet I am afraid it will be public—the advantage of being notorious."

After that, he talked freely, and Sheffield was amazed to learn that the trouble had started in the year 1761, when Gibbon was serving with the militia—thirty-two years previously when he was a young man of twenty-four. At that time he had indeed consulted a surgeon, who, uncertain whether it was the beginning of a rupture or a hydrocele, had asked to see him again, but as the matter had not troubled him he had neglected it then and ever since.

In the middle of November the surgeons operated and removed four quarts of fluid, but it continued to collect, and a fortnight later they removed three more quarts, after which Gibbon felt considerable relief and resumed his social habits— "a delightful day with Burke; an odd one with Monsignor Erskine, the Pope's Nuncio."

He was to spend Christmas at Sheffield Place, and on his way there he visited Lord Auckland's, where he had recently met the Archbishop of Canterbury, of whom he spoke highly. On this occasion he met Pitt, the Prime Minister.

At Sheffield Place his talk was "never more brilliant, nor more entertaining". But before Christmas his appetite began to fail, and fluid collected again in the tumour, so that by the first week of January 1794, it became necessary for him to return to London, where he arrived "half-dead, but not seriously feverish, or ill".

On 13th January a third operation was performed in which six quarts of fluid were discharged. Again he was relieved and confident, saying that even if he was not wholly cured before his return to Lausanne, there was a good surgeon in Geneva who could attend him there.

On the afternoon of the 15th he had a visit from a friend, Craufurd, a Scot. Gibbon told him that he thought himself a good life for ten, twelve, or perhaps twenty years. After that he had the wing of a chicken and three glasses of Madeira.

That evening he was in pain until four in the morning of the 16th, when his stomach was easier. At nine he wanted to get up, but was dissuaded by his valet. At noon, after a visit from the doctor—when he was visibly dying—he took some brandy and water, and died peacefully three-quarters of an hour later. He showed no fear of death, nor is there evidence that he was aware of its approach, for its immediate cause was, not the hydrocele, with which he had hoped to return to Lausanne even if it was not cured, but a displacement in the organs as a result of the third operation, which had set up a peritonitis.

So Gibbon was able to enter into immortality with the same serenity that he had displayed in his mortal life and in his stately progress past the decaying columns of the Roman Empire, *felix opportunitate mortis*; and indeed there was the same felicity in his writings—unity between the Roman of the eighteenth century and the Gibbon who traversed the streets of the Eternal City as a senator in the age of the Antonines.

There is a Chinese saying that the dead are stronger than the living; one that an historian, whose exclusive concern is with the dead, might be expected to cherish. It is true that Gibbon in his first published essay, written in French, undertook the defence of the ancients against the moderns, and always respected the busts, the inscriptions, and the documents of the past, but of death in its more metaphysical aspect he had as little awareness as he had of his own death when he lay dying.

He was a man of this world, but within the limitations of this particular planet, his interests were universal, extending not only over time and place, with a special concern for travels and primitive peoples—"An Iroquois book, even were it full of absurdities, would be an invaluable treasure"—but also into subjects remote from his work. His lively interest in natural history is reflected in the "camelopardalis or Giraffe, the tallest, the most gentle, and the most useless of the large quadrupeds", in "the scaly hide of the rhinoceros", in the dromedaries, and in the Tartar herds of *The Decline and Fall*; he met Buffon in Paris and admired his "sublime genius". He took a rest, to "unbend" his mind after his first volume, in the study of anatomy and chemistry. So too he relaxed after the reign of Justinian to consider the nature of comets, earthquakes, and plagues, before going on to write a masterly account of Roman law.

In this wide range of his interests he was linked to the men of the previous century who had formed the Royal Society, as in his research he was related to the men of the Renaissance who had quarried so diligently in the ruins of Rome. He could even adopt their laments over mortality, though only from a political standpoint, as in a letter on the collapse of French institutions: "They are crumbled into dust; they are vanished from the earth." Yet it is noteworthy that when the last chapter of *The Decline and Fall* gave him his best opportunity for such laments, he let it pass; there was "ample scope for moralising on the vicissitudes of fortune, which spares neither man nor the proudest of his works, which buries empires and cities in a common grave" (vii, p. 313), but he was content with a quotation and himself proceeded to an exact estimate of the material damage. Unlike the men of the Renaissance, he was not haunted by the presence of death and skulls. If they had stood betwen the Tree of Life and the Tree of Knowledge, he had already made the choice of knowledge, and in abandoning Christianity he also abandoned any concern with the other world.

In this he was more akin to the writers of the French Enlightenment than to the empirical English, who could retain a "constitutional" religion as they preserved a constitutional monarchy, refraining from hostilities and remaining in diplomatic relations with the other world. Yet he was English enough in resisting essential changes, and if there was ironical exaggeration in his defence of the Lisbon Inquisition after the outbreak of the French Revolution, it is at least certain that he had no desire to construct either a new republic or an earthly paradise; his golden age was in the past. If this difference between looking backwards to the past and forwards to the future is the true distinction between conservatives and progressives, then Gibbon was a thorough conservative, remote from the later French Enlightenment.

He drew more largely from the earlier Enlightenment in the Low Countries, especially the scholarly Le Clerc. Yet his greatest debt as an historian was to the austere Jansenist Tillemont, whose *Mémoires ecclésiastiques* and *Histoire des empereurs* paved his Roman road through the first five centuries and into the sixth. He acknowledged this debt to Tillemont in his *Autobiography* (p. 172), when speaking of "the collections of Tillemont, whose inimitable accuracy almost assumes the character of genius", and again in a footnote in Chapter XLVII of *The Decline and Fall* when he took leave of "that incomparable guide". Yet perhaps the best indication of his debt to Tillemont is the superiority of his own first three volumes to the last three. The scattered nature of his later summaries and the omissions in his Byzantine history might have been remedied by a guide of Tillemont's calibre.

It is ironic that it was the piety of Port-Royal which gave

most to his history in Tillemont and to his style in Pascal—a debt also acknowledged in his *Autobiography* (p. 75). It further reveals that, unlike Voltaire, he valued scholarship above the polemics of the Enlightenment.

His reputation as a progressive and as a man of the Enlightenment depends largely on his attitude to religion. But while there is little doubt that he had come to regard all religion, other than a shadowy deism, as superstition, here too his mind was directed to the past, not to the future. It was as a historian that he wrote of Christianity, exposing the legends, the pious fancies, the misrepresentations and the injustices which had resulted less from a false view of religion than from a pure ignorance of history. Some of the ecclesiastical chroniclers who most aroused his sarcasm had aimed at strengthening the faith of their readers more than at increasing their knowledge of history. Their history was sometimes fiction because they were in fact more like novelists, writing to create a particular impression or to evoke a special emotion. But Gibbon had as firm a belief in the truth of history as they had in the truth of religion, to which he was as indifferent as they were to history. It was on historical, not on religious, grounds that he attacked them, and he was right in claiming that he was attached to no party but concerned only with "the candour of history". It was inevitable, in view of his ironical style and his scepticism, that he should also express his own doubts on religion itself, but this was only an indirect result of his method: his first purpose was the writing of authentic history.

Apart from vindicating this method, he avoided controversy, and he was as critical of those who wrote history from a partisan angle as he was of the Christian chroniclers, even calling Voltaire a "bigot". In this he was distinguished from the general eighteenth-century reaction against Christianity, which was a moral and a political movement, culminating in the French Revolution with its overthrow of former moral and political standards. This was provoked by corruption and decay in Church and State, evident in England no less than in France; but neither aroused Gibbon's resentment. If he railed against "the monks of Oxford", it was more for their neglect of scholarship than for the fatness of their livings, while he was so little opposed to laxity in the State as to accept a sinecure for himself in becoming a Lord of Trade. Even in his scepticism he was not a propagandist, for he regarded this as the aristo-cratic attitude of "a few inquisitive minds"; for the multitude he was content with "useful prejudices combating on the side of national manners".

His mission was not to renew the face of the earth, but to describe the world of appearances and the real facts of its recorded history. It was this ideal independence which gave a unique quality to his style. In his *Autobiography* (p. 1) he observed that "style is the image of character", and that "the style of an author should be the image of his mind". (p. 177.) Nobly he obeyed his own precept, for his style was the perfect mirror of his serenity.

In this serenity Gibbon is as great a master of English prose as is Pope of English verse, and it was natural that in the century following his own, which issued in the Romantic movement, his style should be as little appreciated as Pope's. In the European tradition, which balances between Jewish inspiration, with its visions of heaven, and Roman discipline with its roads on earth, he was emphatically a Roman. It is significant that when Byron and Shelley visited his garden in Lausanne, it was Byron, the admirer of Pope, who gathered some acacia leaves in honour of Gibbon, while the visionary Shelley refrained, reflecting on "the greater and more sacred name of Rousseau", who had disapproved of Gibbon as a lover for Suzanne and who contributed so much to the formation of Romantic sensibility.

The nineteenth century, with its national and democratic movements, its Romantic literature, its love of legend, its romantic conception of love, its respect for individual emotions and despairs and its increasing distrust of aristocracy, moved away from Gibbon and his world. Historians respected his scholarship, but by the end of the century they were already turning from narrative to the history of ideas and the comparison of cultures. This led even the most secular historians to estimate religion less as an ecclesiastical institution than as a deep human impulse beyond Gibbon's doubtful balancing of motives. Religion itself had changed since the eighteenth century, revived first by the Romantic nostalgia for the ages of faith, then by the Oxford Movement and the Catholic Romantics in the German lands, and braced by attacks made on it in France, Germany, and Italy; while in such countries as Ireland and Poland the Church herself supplied "the banners of the people".

Finally, the twentieth century fought two great wars which shattered Gibbon's "great republic" of Europe, removed it from the leadership of the civilized world, destroyed the conception of aristocracy and abolished most of those "old establishments" which the French Revolution had inclined him to cherish, while in Russia and the Balkans a new culture emerged from the lands of that Byzantine Empire which he had so despised.

Today historians and their readers are more interested in the decline and fall of Europe than in that of the Roman Empire. Yet it is perhaps today, and precisely for that reason, that Gibbon is read with more interest than ever before, because he presents so lucid a picture of what happens in the disruption of civilization and the emergence of a new world.

Today Gibbon is read not only as an evocation of the past but as a history of the present.

Historians, whether Americans or Europeans, Catholics or Communists, democrats or conservatives, cannot write the history of their own times, not only because they lack the justice and the perspective of history, but because their own hopes and fears come between them and the truth. Perhaps it is even impossible for historians to see clearly into the past without distortion. Even Gibbon's "candour" was only a vision seen in the light of his loyalty to the Roman Empire and to the "great republic" of Europe. But the simplicity and the coherence of that vision, the serenity of his observation, raised his work above the level of those who, whether on religious, national, or political grounds, were more involved in the details or the debates of the past. There are other interpretations of European history, but there is none in English presented with such clarity or with such unity.

Gibbon stood only for the framework of the European tradition, the Roman virtues of discipline and classical order, its bones and bodily structure. Its spirit, its Jewish and Christian inspiration, were remote from him, as was the Greek philosophy which it had adapted to its expression. He preferred reason to emotion, and both in his personal life and in his writing he valued serenity more than the impulses of the heart. Yet he had experienced this other inspiration in his youth, as he had also felt the influence of love. His rejection of them moulded more than it warped his character. If he had regretted them, he would hardly have returned to Lausanne, where he had experienced them, nor found there the tranquillity of his later life. It was his destiny as a historian to devote himself to the Roman reality and close his mind to other inspirations.

He ignored the world of spirits, but nothing in the world of appearances was too remote for his ceaseless investigation. His weakness was that of history itself, which unrolls its proud record of persons and places, but is incapable of rising from the dead or infusing them with the breath of life. History is not even the crime and folly to which Gibbon consigned it, for they at least have life in them; history is a cemetery, a place of broken columns and statues such as Gibbon saw as a young man in Rome, ruins which inspired him to set before them his magnificent and florid inscriptions.

Yet there is one gate of life into this cemetery, one power which can make the dead bones live. Those who are relations of the dead and those who are inspired by the same passions as inspired them can find some life among the tombstones. Sons salute their fathers, lovers embrace their dead mistresses, Christians share the joy and agony of their martyrs. Gibbon too found among the graves those imperial and senatorial figures whom he could respect in his own day. He penetrated into the Roman past and uncovered there the noble features of the eighteenth century. Nor was this a vision mortified by time. There is a human greatness which survives the ages, men worthy of the laurel which has the permanence of stone. Such men were the Antonines. Such too was Athanasius, to whom Gibbon more generously extended his tribute. Even in the cemetery of history Gibbon could still discern the living traits of a man.

Those other mysteries of the past, love and religion, which are also mysteries of the present, eluded him among the shades as they also escaped him in the bright daylight of his own life. But he saw enough to raise some statues from the dead, and it is glory enough for any writer that he can turn a living sun to light the mortal darkness of the past.

NOTE ON SOURCES

THIS study has been largely based, as will be all too evident to those familiar with Gibbon material, on relating his *Autobiography* to *The Decline and Fall of the Roman Empire*, both of which are universally accessible in a number of editions. Here the *Autobiography* has been quoted in the World's Classics edition of the Oxford University Press (1950), *The Decline and Fall* in Bury's edition, 7 vols. (1926–9).

The best biography of Gibbon, both in style and research, is D. M. Low's *Edward Gibbon* (Chatto and Windus, 1937). There are shorter lives by G. M. Young (Peter Davies, 1932), and by Michael Joyce (Longmans, 1953). Yet Cotter Morison's *Gibbon* in the "English Men of Letters" series (Macmillan, 1878), still has a unique contribution to make, both in appreciation of Gibbon's work and character, owing to the writer's special sympathy for his subject.

The Letters of Edward Gibbon, edited by J. E. Norton (Cassell, 1956), is a monumental edition in three volumes, a model of its type.

Gibbon's *Miscellaneous Writings*, London, 1837, includes extracts from his Journal.

For information on and access to the work of Robert Persons, I am indebted to the Rev. Leo Hicks, S. J.

On the French eighteenth century and climate of opinion, the first volume of Sorel's *L'Europe et la révolution française* retains its mastery.

Recent historians who have illuminated Gibbon's period or presented a wider view of the Byzantine Empire include

GIBBON AND ROME

Christopher Dawson, Steven Runciman, and Geoffrey Barra-clough.

The Root of Europe (Chatto and Windus, 1952) is a short, but scholarly and richly illustrated symposium of Greek and Byzantine influences on European history.

Byzantium into Europe, by Jack Lindsay (Bodley Head, 1952), has the interest of a fresh view from a Communist angle.

The Everyman edition of *The Decline and Fall* has not only the very striking introduction by Christopher Dawson, but a considerable bibliography on Gibbon, on his authorities, and on later historical works.

INDEX

INDEX

PASCAL, 92, 190
Pater, Walter, 11
Pavilliard, 52ff
Persons, Robert, 47, 48, 56
Pitt, 122, 186
Plato, 162
Pope, 119, 191
Porson, 65, 121, 122
Porten, Catherine, 24, 26, 64

QUENNELL, PETER, 122

REYNOLDS, SIR JOSHUA, 85, 111
Robertson, 119
Rousseau, 69, 91, 139
Runciman, Steven, 165

SAINTSBURY, GEORGE, 41, 118
Sheffield, Lord, 49, 99, 109, 148, 178,
    182, 184, 185

Sheridan, 8, 159
Smeaton, Oliphant, 180
Sterne, 137
Swift, 81, 137

TACITUS, 8
Tillemont, 108, 189
Toynbee, Arnold, 170

VESPASIAN, 101, 103
Voltaire, 91, 92

WALPOLE, HORACE, 137, 163
Walpole, Sir Robert, 23
Warburton, Bishop, 108
Ward, Sir A. W., 111, 142
Wesley, John, 37, 138

YOUNG, G. M., 9, 122